P9-CJF-357

THE SPORTING CHEF'S
Better Venison
COOKBOOK

SCOTT LEYSATH

Copyright ©2012 Scott Leysath

All rights reserved. No portion of this publication may be reproduced or transmitted in any form or by any means, electronic or mechanical, including photocopy, recording, or any information storage and retrieval system, without permission in writing from the publisher, except by a reviewer who may quote brief passages in a critical article or review to be printed in a magazine or newspaper, or electronically transmitted on radio, television, or the Internet.

Published by

Krause Publications, a division of F+W, A Content + eCommerce Company
700 East State Street • Iola, WI 54990-0001
715-445-2214 • 888-457-2873
www.krausebooks.com

To order books or other products call toll-free 1-800-258-0929,
or visit us online at www.shopdeerhunting.com

All photography by Kate McElvoy

ISBN-13: 978-1-4402-3457-6
ISBN-10: 1-4402-3457-4

Cover Design by Dustin Reid
Designed by Jana Tappa
Edited by Brian Lovett

Printed in the United States of America

To Janell, Jake and all my four-legged companions.
I may be out in the woods, but I'll always leave
a garlic scent trail behind.

Table of Contents

Soups & Stews

On the Grill

In the Oven

Stovetop

Smoking

Introduction

This cookbook is a collection of my favorite venison recipes. These are kitchen-tested dishes I've prepared many times the past few decades. They have proven to be popular, delicious and user-friendly. The ones with the shortest list of ingredients and instructions are typically the ones you will use most often. Please, use my recipes as an outline and a starting point. Eventually, you should leave the measuring spoons in the drawer and eyeball the ingredients. You can always adjust the seasonings at the end.

I'll assume that most of you have probably spent some time deer hunting and hopefully have shot and cooked a deer or two. Others might not have the desire to shoot a deer, but they're stuck doing the cooking. If you want to know the proper way to field-dress a deer, there are several great resources, online and in print. This book won't help.

Food and cooking has never been more popular. For many years, there were only a handful of TV chefs. Graham Kerr, Julia Child, Justin Wilson and Jacques Pépin showed us how to cook beyond the casserole, meatloaf and pot roast. The TV Food Network (later, just Food Network) changed everything. Restaurant chefs became celebrities, and the public learned how to pronounce chipotle. I've had the good fortune to be able to earn a decent living doing one of the things I love the most — cooking fish and game. Without Emeril Lagasse, I'd probably still be running restaurants and catering businesses.

Although most TV cooking shows look pretty much the same, I haven't seen any indication they are on the decline. Many, usually with a competitive angle, have moved from cable to prime-time mainstream TV. Home cooks and pro chefs battle to see who can make the most of a pile of ingredients that most of us, including me, have never heard of. I'm all for the pursuit of something new, but I'd prefer to pursue a deer or turkey than the next food fad. Recipes that are simple to prepare, don't require a long list of obscure ingredients and, most important, taste really good will be in use long after herbal foams have evaporated. Molecular gastronomy is interesting, but I'd rather go fishing.

I'm not a "foodie," but I am passionate about cooking, especially when it comes to anything with fur, fins or feathers. However, my favorite foods are those that don't require any cooking at all. Sashimi, homegrown tomatoes and chilled, briny oysters are good or they're not. You can't dress up a bad oyster or raw piece of fish, nor should you try. Honestly, I get tired of eating most things and need to mix up my menus. Too much of a good thing, I suppose. I meet people who apparently don't get worn out on a short list of edible critters and claim to live solely on animals they have harvested themselves. At some point, they are going to need a few new recipes.

This book is a blend of flavorful and easy recipes that you'll use all the time and others that are a bit more time-consuming. Although I'm all for free-ranging, organic ingredients and naturally occurring plants and animals, the only thing that's truly free-range in this book is the venison. I'm not trying to "outchef" anyone, just to provide recipes that I hope you'll use again and again. Nothing makes me happier than a cookbook full of food stains, especially if the recipes are my own.

A FEW THOUGHTS ON RECIPES AND COOKING

- I've had the opportunity to visit many hunting and fishing lodges and clubs. I'm amused at the number of containers of meat tenderizers in the pantry. If you want your game to be tender, proper field care, aging, storage and cooking is the key, not something out of a bottle.

- I use kosher salt or sea salt. Some of the recipes in this book list just "salt." Use your own discretion, and season with salt to taste. If a recipe specifies a particular type of salt, such as kosher salt, and all you have is table salt, use about three-fourths of the quantity listed in the recipe. Fine-ground table salt is denser than kosher salt. In general, if you use table salt instead of kosher salt, use a little less. You can always add more. When incorporated into a recipe, I can't tell the difference between salts, but there is a distinct flavor and texture difference when sprinkled over a finished dish.

- I don't have anything against injecting venison roasts with marinades. Many of my friends swear there's no better way to season a roast. It sounds a little goofy, but I prefer to marinade venison roasts after they're cooked. When meat is uncooked, marinades won't penetrate much beyond the outside 1/4 inch. Jabbing them with a fork or hand tenderizer will help marinade work its way into the meat, but it'll take a while to get there. When meat is hot and cooked, it is much more porous. Take a hot, slightly undercooked roast, and place it into the smallest cooler in which it will fit. Douse it with a room-temperature marinade, and give it a toss to coat. Keep the air space to a minimum. If necessary, place a layer of heavy-duty foil over the meat, and fold up a clean towel over the foil to help retain the heat. The hot meat will absorb the marinade much more readily than raw meat. Leave the roast in the marinade for an hour or so, and you'll be amazed at how much more flavor is imparted to the meat. As tempting as it might be, do not open the lid of the cooler for at least 45 minutes. Allowing the heat to escape will cool off the meat, and the marinade can't do its job. I do the same thing with a wild or domestic turkey. After two hours in a cooler, the bird is still very hot and extremely moist.

- Pepper isn't just pepper. Freshly ground pepper has more flavor. When a recipe calls for pepper, the choice is yours whether you use freshly ground or already ground pepper. I rarely use old pepper that's already ground.

- Garlic out of a jar might be convenient, but it doesn't taste like freshly minced whole garlic cloves. If you must use it, double the quantity specified in a recipe.

- Wipe venison dry before seasoning or cooking. Deer blood won't improve the flavor of the meat. Note how much bloody liquid runs out of a thawed piece of venison. Use two-ply paper or cloth towels to leach the liquid away from the meat. When dry, rub with a thin coating of olive oil and your favorite seasoning.

- Meat needs to rest before and after cooking. Remove venison steaks from the refrigerator 10 to 15 minutes before cooking so the internal temperature is about the same as the outside. When a refrigerated deer steak is placed directly onto a grill, the juices will be more concentrated, sort of, in the cold center. They're not really compressed into the center, but the more-cooked outside of the meat isn't able to retain the juices as readily as the lesser-cooked center. When the meat is cooked to the desired temperature, hopefully not beyond medium-rare, it should rest for several minutes to give the juices a chance to redistribute to the outer edges as they cool. When you cut into a deer steak that's fresh off the grill, the juices will run out across the plate. If you let it rest for five to 10 minutes before slicing, most of the juice will remain distributed within the meat.

- Contrary to what the TV chefs tell us, searing meat on the outside does not "seal in the juices." It does, however, make it taste better. Charred venison steaks have more flavor and texture than those cooked at lower temperatures, but the seared outside does not create an impenetrable coating.

- Standard-grade aluminum foil should be illegal. Wrapping a smoked or grilled venison roast with cheap, thin foil will result in torn foil that won't retain heat and will allow juices, sauces and marinades to escape. At half the price of heavy-duty foil, it's not worth it.

- One pound of raw meat equals about 2 cups. Often recipes specify quantity of meat based on weight. Because venison doesn't come in a package and most people don't weigh their ingredients, this is good to know. I own a food scale and use if fairly often.

- Venison should be trimmed of most visible sinew, gristle, fascia, silver skin and anything that's not muscle. Freezing the meat for an hour will make it easier to remove the junk with a sharp, thin-bladed knife.

- Why olive oil? For most recipes, any decent-quality, neutral oil will work. I buy cheap olive oil in large gallon jugs and burn through it quickly. Extra-virgin olive oils have a deeper, richer flavor. They're also more expensive. I use the good stuff when I want the flavor of olive oil to come through in a sauce or vinaigrette.

- I often use dry seasoning in my recipes. Many years ago, I did a radio interview to promote my first cookbook. The host and I were discussing recipes that included an abundance of fresh herbs. We took a call from an irritated listener from Fairbanks, Alaska, who didn't see a lot of fresh basil or rosemary. Although I prefer fresh herbs and have a hillside of them at home, I know many home cooks rely on the dried stuff in the pantry. Remember that dried herbs lose their potency through time.

- When adding fresh herbs to a recipe, add more delicate herbs near the end of the cooking part. Fresh basil, cilantro or parsley will disintegrate while stewing in a sauce. Added right before finishing the dish, the flavor of the fresh herbs will be infinitely more vibrant. Hardier herbs such as rosemary, sage and thyme can be added earlier on in the cooking process.

- "What's with all the garlic?" is a question I hear often. I like garlic. If you don't like it as much as me, leave it out, or use less than the recipe calls for. Likewise, if you're not a fan of spicy dishes, leave out the spicy part of a recipe, and it will still taste good.

- After you've let your cooked venison rest for several minutes, slice it across the grain before serving. Cutting across the grain, or muscle fibers, will make the meat much more tender. Try it yourself. Cut a piece of cooked venison across and with the grain. Try pulling the meat apart with moderate pressure. The meat cut across the grain will be much more tender. If your sliced venison has lines running through it, it's been cut with the grain and will be chewier.

chapter 1

Venison Cooking Basics

Tips and techniques to make any venison dish taste its best.

FIELD CARE, TRANSPORTATION AND STORAGE

It kills me when I see dead deer being driven around in the back of a truck or, even worse, strapped to the hood or roof of a car. I got it. You shot a deer, and the rest of the world wants to know about it. But really, they don't. Oh sure, it might be freezing cold outside — that will help — but there's no substitute for proper field-dressing and transportation. The longer you wait to field-dress, completely cool, wrap and transport your deer to wherever it is going to be processed, the greater the risk of contamination and spoilage.

If you're a relatively successful deer hunter, I'm sure you've enjoyed cooked venison that might have been left in the field overnight or took hours to get back to the truck on a hot day, and it tasted just fine. I know that you've also eaten deer that didn't taste quite right.

"You know, this deer's got a little gamey taste to it. I think it mighta been eating, I don't know, sagebrush or something."

Oh, well. Next time, you'll need to soak it in something powerful for a few days. That'll do it.

Why not eliminate as many variables as possible? If you've done everything right to get your deer into cold storage quickly, it will greatly increase the chances that it will taste great at the dinner table.

HOW LONG TO AGE A DEER

I've endured many arguments about aging deer before processing. Here's the bottom line, at least for me: Hang your deer for at least 24 hours. That's about how long it takes for the animal to go through rigor mortis, the chemical change that muscles undergo before they eventually loosen up. The tender muscles, such as tenderloins and backstraps, can be excised from a fresh kill and cooked immediately with OK results, but both will benefit from waiting a day or so, after the muscle contraction from rigor mortis has passed.

After the first 24 hours, a young deer can be butchered immediately, but a couple of more days of hanging will make the animal more tender when cooked, assuming that the deer hangs in a controlled-temperature locker of 33 to 40 degrees. If it's too cold, the enzymes that break down the muscle tissue can't do their work. If it's too warm,

You shot a deer, and the rest of the world wants to know about it. But really, they don't.

bacteria moves in and has its way with the meat, making it spoil. You'll probably notice the smell. If you can't control the temperature at home, send it to a locker for processing or, at the least, to hang for a few days before you process it yourself. If you don't have room for a refrigerated storage locker at home, but enough for a spare refrigerator in the garage, consider picking up a good used fridge for aging your deer. Butcher the animal into hindquarters, shoulders and other parts, and age it in the refrigerator.

Older animals can use a few more days to age properly, but extended aging will also give the venison a more pronounced, stronger flavor when cooked. One week to 10 days is usually plenty of time for an average deer to dry age, although I have a few friends who swear by aging deer for two to three weeks. The also douse everything with hot sauce.

DEER PARTS AND HOW TO COOK THEM

Tenderloins are so named because they're, um, tender. They sit inside the body cavity and just go along for the ride. Tenderloins don't work much, and consequently, they're very tender when cooked. It hurts me to see someone cook any tenderloin, deer or otherwise, past medium-rare. If you order a well-done filet mignon in a restaurant, know that the cooks are saying unflattering things about you. Rub them with olive oil, salt and pepper, and cook for a few minutes per side. That's plenty.

You won't find anything labeled "backstrap" in a grocery store meat case. It's the loin of a deer. Located on the outside of either side of the backbone, it's tender, but not as tender as the tenderloin, although many people mistakenly refer to it by the same name. Think of the meaty part of a T-bone steak or pork chop. The backstrap of a younger animal is more tender than that of an old buck. They are most often butterflied by game processors, ready to season and sear in a skillet or on a hot grill. They can be stuffed and tied as whole muscles or individual steaks. Overcooking will, in my opinion, ruin them. If your backstrap is tough and chewy, it's probably just because it has been overcooked. Because the steaks are about the size and shape of a beef tender-loin, they are often wrapped with bacon, giving them fat and flavor. Backstraps are best cooked over high or medium-high heat. If you put them into a slow-cooker with a can of cream of mushroom soup, please don't tell anyone.

Neck and shoulder roasts are sinewy, tough hunks of meat that require extended cooking, preferably along with enough liquid to help break down the muscles with steam heat. Boning out a neck roast is crazy. It's mostly bone, and you won't end up with much meat in the end. I feel the same way about front shoulders. Rub neck and shoulder roasts with your favorite rub, stick them in the fridge for a day or so, brown them, and braise them in a shallow bath of stock and the trimmed ends of whatever vegetables you have on hand. In about six to eight hours, the meat will fall off the bone of the shoulder roast. When done, the bone will pull away from the meat cleanly, leav-ing behind moist, tender chunks of meat, devoid of silver skin and sinew. Shoulder meat can be trimmed off the bone and ground into burger, too, but I prefer the braising method. Less time in the kitchen means more time in the field.

Shanks, the bottom muscle of the legs, are really tough and stringy, but when cooked properly, they are every bit as good as braised veal or lamb shanks. Like the shoulder and neck roasts, they must be cooked slowly with some form of liquid until they almost fall off the bone. Substitute the veal shanks from any osso buco recipe with deer shanks, and the result will be the same — very tender, moist, flavorful shanks that beg for a side of creamy mashed potatoes or polenta to help soak up the pan sauce. As with any slow-cooking method, the work is done by the oven. Other than chopping a few vegetables and opening a can of tomato product, you don't have to do much except smell the aroma and savor the flavor. It beats the heck out of grinding the trimmed meat into burger. The shanks from very small deer can be browned and used to make stock. Do not throw them away.

I take great pride in fooling others into thinking that I'm serving them backstraps when, really, they're eating trimmed hindquarter or rump muscles. All too often, game processors simply turn large hindquarter muscle groups into roasts. Although I enjoy a good venison roast, I'm more likely to remove each muscle from each leg by running a sharp boning knife around the sinews that binds the individual muscles together. If the animal was old, I use a handheld tenderizing gizmo like a Jaccard to break through the

How you slice any of the hindquarter muscles after cooking will make a huge difference on how it behaves between your teeth.

muscle fibers, making the cooked meat much less chewy. Big deer will benefit from at least a few hours in a marinade of olive oil, garlic, salt and pepper. Using overpowering marinades that claim to make venison taste like something other than venison isn't for me. I prefer to enhance rather than cover up the taste of deer meat.

How you slice any of the hindquarter muscles after cooking will make a huge difference on how it behaves between your teeth. After cooking, slice the meat across the grain, cutting through the muscle fibers, for venison that is tender to the bite. Scraps and trim from your hindquarter butchering can be used for soups, stews or ground into burger.

Any other parts of a deer — flanks, rib meat and more — can be ground or stewed. Many of us irresponsibly waste way too much usable meat. The way I see it, we've invested a great deal of time and money to get the deer home, so it seems silly to discard otherwise edible parts. Although I'm not a big fan of the taste of venison fat, I've sampled some rendered fat from corn-fed deer, and it's just fine.

How I decide which recipe or method of cooking I'm going to use depends on how the deer behaves in the pan. Cut a thin piece of meat across the grain of any trimmed piece of venison. Lightly coat with olive oil, salt and pepper and quickly brown to medium-rare in a hot skillet. Taste it. If it's tender and mild, you're good to grill, pan sear or broil. If it's tough and chewy, it's going to need some help either by pounding with a mallet or heavy skillet to break down the tough muscle or by tenderizing with a Jaccard or fork. Place it in a marinade of olive oil, balsamic vinegar, garlic, salt and pepper for 12 hours or more. Then try the quick-fire test again. Most likely, it will be much more tender. If not, you probably have a slow-cooking, braising or stewing candidate. If the meat is off-tasting, it might be trying to tell you something. If it smells spoiled, I don't eat it.

SAFE AT ANY TEMPERATURE?

This is another topic for debate, but I eat better cuts of venison on the rare to medium-rare side, usually not cooked beyond an internal temperature of 135 degrees. Assuming that the outside part of a backstrap, tenderloin or hindquarter steak has not come in contact with any contaminant, such as fecal matter, I'm confident that my meat is safe to eat at any temperature. How you decide to cook your venison is simply a matter of personal choice, but if you've always eaten it well-done for whatever reason, I'd really like you to consider trying just a bite of a medium-rare piece of deer meat. What's the worst that could happen?

Many years ago, I began my wild-game cooking demonstrations and seminars by eating a raw slice of venison. Several of the attendees reeled in horror, and a few even left the room with the probable assumption that anyone who would eat a raw piece of deer wasn't worth a listen. I stopped doing it, not because I feared for my health, but because I really got tired of eating raw meat. I also seared a few slices of hindquarter steaks and dunked them in a dark sauce before offering up a sample to those who claimed that venison is tough and gamey. The sauce disguised the fact that the meat was actually just a little purple in the center and cooked somewhere between rare and medium-rare. It changed the minds of most folks who decided long ago that venison tasted awful. They'd ask, "What did you do to make it so tender?" The answer is to not overcook it.

Ground venison has a higher probability of coming in contact with contaminants, and there are documented cases of people coming in contact with and getting very sick from E. coli bacteria. E. coli dies at 160 degrees. If you want to avoid it, cook your ground meat to an internal temperature of 160 degrees. The same thing goes for any piece of meat, wild or domestic. If you cook meat long enough, it'll kill just about anything that could harm you. I'm still going to take extra care when processing the meat and cook primal cuts closer to rare than well-done.

Other region-specific factors, such as chronic wasting disease, should be considered before processing your animal, especially when you start messing around with the brain, eyes, spleen, tonsils, lymph nodes or spinal cord —deer parts that I haven't had any trouble avoiding contact with. Again, how you cook your deer is entirely up to you. If you're worried about any health issues from ingesting lesser-cooked venison, do the research, and decide for yourself.

PACKAGING AND STORAGE

There's nothing like pulling a piece of venison backstrap out of the freezer, only to discover that a good part of it is freezer-burned. You can trim away the discolored parts, and the rest is fine to cook and eat, but why waste any of it? Keeping your venison from going south in the freezer is a no-brainer.

The absolute best way to keep any game properly frozen is with a vacuum-packaging system. If you decide to go that route, I'd highly recommend that you avoid a cheap one. They don't last long and need to rest between vacuum sessions. Plan on spending at least $150 for a unit that will keep up with a successful deer season.

Of course, you probably won't be able to fit a deer hindquarter into a vacuum bag. First, wrap it tightly and carefully with plastic wrap. The heavier the plastic wrap, the better. Then wrap it a few times with butcher paper, again keeping out as much air space as possible. Tape it and label the package, not the tape, with the date and specific cut of deer.

Freezer-safe zipper lock bags will suffice, but they are no substitute for vacuum-packaging. Double-bag them, squeezing out as much air as possible before dating and labeling the outside with a permanent marker.

Meat does not get better with age when frozen. No matter how you package it, it's always best when eaten today, not three years down the road. Get in the habit of cleaning out your freezer before the next season begins. Invite friends over for a venison feast to get them in the mood for this year's hunt. Sharing the fruits of the harvest is a big part of the reason we spend days in a frozen tree stand. Besides, it sure beats doing yard work or shopping.

chapter two

Small Bites

Picture yourself standing around a smoky grill after a productive day in the field, chomping on a hot, two-bite morsel, most likely wrapped in bacon. It sets the stage for the game feast to come. Of course, you can make a meal out of a mess of appetizers, and why not?

I've lost count of how many game chefs have shared the same recipe. You know, the one where the strips of meat are marinated for a day or two before getting wrapped in jalapeño, some form of cheese and bacon. I've had people tell me, "It doesn't even taste like deer!" as if that was a victory. I know it tastes great, but the world really doesn't need a repeat of the same recipe. Don't think I'm getting on my culinary high horse; I make the old bacon-wrapped deer thing myself. It really is good.

Backstrap, Smoked Oyster, Green Onion and Bacon Snack

An alternative to the usual bacon-wrapped venison-on-a-toothpick recipe, this one combines smoky canned oysters, scallions and, of course, bacon. Also, try it with fresh, "unsmoked" medium-sized oysters, preferably from Apalachicola, Fla. — home of the world's best oysters. Partially cooking the bacon before wrapping will keep the meat from overcooking while waiting for the bacon to get fully cooked.

4 to 6 appetizer servings

INGREDIENTS

- 16 to 20 thin slices from the backstrap, cutting across the grain into wide pieces
- salt and pepper
- 16 to 20 canned smoked oysters
- 16 to 20 green onions, green part only
- 16 to 20 strips thin-sliced bacon, partially cooked (about halfway)
- 16 to 20 small wooden skewers, soaked in water for 30 minutes

1. Place bacon strips on a flat surface. For each appetizer, wrap green onion around oyster, and place oyster in the center of the meat. Roll meat around oyster and green onion, and place on one end of the bacon. Roll bacon snugly around meat, and secure with skewer.
2. Place on a medium-hot grill or under a broiler until bacon is crisp.

Prosciutto, Mango and Jalapeño Bites

A variation on the standard bacon-wrapped deer recipe.

4 to 6 appetizer servings

INGREDIENTS

- 16 to 20 ½-inch-wide by 3-inch-long strips of venison
- ¼ cup olive oil
- 1 tablespoon sesame oil
- ¼ cup soy sauce
- ¼ cup rice vinegar
- 2 tablespoons orange marmalade
- 1 teaspoon freshly ground black pepper
- 1 tablespoon Tabasco
- 1 to 2 slightly underripe mangoes
- 4 jalapeño peppers
- 16 to 20 very thin slices prosciutto
- small wooden skewers, soaked in water for 30 minutes

1. Combine olive oil in a bowl with next 6 ingredients. Add meat, cover and marinate for 2 to 3 hours. Remove meat from marinade, and pat dry with paper towels.

2. Peel and seed mango, and cut into strips, about the same size as the venison. Slice around the outside of the jalapeño peppers, removing the outside green part and leaving the inside seeds, ribs and stem intact. Discard seed and stem centers. Each unseeded pepper will yield 4 to 5 slices, about ¾ inch wide.

3. Lay prosciutto on a flat surface. Starting at the end of each slice, place a piece of mango, a slice of jalapeño pepper and a piece of marinated venison across the prosciutto. Wrap snugly, and secure with a skewer. Grill or broil until prosciutto is just a tad crispy and meat is medium-rare.

Goat Cheese "Pâté"

Tasia Malakasis, of the famous Belle Chevre Fromagerie near Athens, Ala., showed me how to make this delicious pâté-like spread out of any cooked game meat, and it only takes a few minutes to whip up a batch.

Makes about 2 cups

INGREDIENTS

- 3 strips bacon, diced
- ¼ cup onion, finely minced
- 1 clove garlic, minced
- 1⅓ cups venison backstrap or tenderized hindquarter cut, trimmed of silver skin and gristle and diced into ½-inch cubes
- ⅓ cup roasted pistachios or almonds
- ⅓ cup dried cranberries (or Craisins)
- ½ cup goat cheese
- 2 tablespoons fresh parsley leaves, minced
- 1 teaspoon freshly squeezed lemon juice
- salt and pepper to taste

1. Lightly brown bacon in a large skillet over medium heat. Add onion, garlic and diced venison, and sauté until meat is just cooked and not overcooked. Allow to cool.

2. Place pistachios and cranberries in a food processor, and process until smooth. Add cooled venison mixture, and pulse until smooth. Add goat cheese, parsley and lemon juice, and continue processing until mixture is creamy and smooth. Season with salt and pepper.

3. Serve with crackers or toast points.

Fireballs

These are like small, bite-sized meatballs, only hotter. The heat comes from the Sriracha, a Southeast Asian hot sauce often called "rooster sauce" because of the drawing of a rooster on the label of a popular brand. Look in the Asian section of your market for any product labeled Chili-Garlic, Sambal or Asian Hot Sauce. Start with a drop or two, and keep adding hot sauce until you get to your preferred level of heat.

6 to 8 appetizer servings

INGREDIENTS

- 1 pound ground venison
- ¼ pound ground pork
- ½ teaspoon fresh ginger, peeled and minced
- 3 cloves garlic, minced
- 3 green onions, minced
- 1 egg, beaten
- ½ teaspoon sesame oil
- ¼ teaspoon salt
- Sriracha (hot chili sauce) to taste
- toothpicks

1. In a bowl, combine all ingredients except Sriracha. Use your (clean) hands to mix ingredients thoroughly. Form some of the mixture into a ball, about ¾ the size of a golf ball, and press together. The mixture should be a little moist while holding together with mild pressure. If it falls apart easily, add some breadcrumbs as a binder.

2. Form the mixture into balls, and place on a lightly greased baking pan. Place in a preheated 375-degree oven until evenly browned, about 8 to 10 minutes. Place a small dollop of Sriracha on the top of each meatball, and stab with toothpick.

Stuffed Mushrooms

This is a tasty way to use up ground venison, something many successful deer hunters seem to have in abundance. I usually end up with more stuffing than I have mushrooms to stuff, which makes for a great little snack while the mushrooms are in the oven. When it comes to ground antlered game, use your imagination. Any recipe that calls for ground beef or pork can be used for ground venison.

16 servings

INGREDIENTS

- 16 medium mushrooms
- 3 tablespoons butter
- 3 tablespoons red bell pepper (or any color)
- 2 garlic cloves, minced
- 1¼ cups ground venison
- 1 tablespoon Italian seasoning
- ¼ cup breadcrumbs
- pinch red pepper flakes
- ½ cup shredded mozzarella cheese
- salt and pepper to taste

1. Remove stems from mushrooms, and scoop out dark brown "gills" with a teaspoon while keeping the mushroom cap intact. Preheat oven to 400 degrees.

2. Melt butter in a large skillet over medium heat. Add pepper and garlic, and sauté for 2 to 3 minutes. Add venison and Italian seasoning, and sauté until just cooked. Cool mixture.

3. In a medium bowl, combine cooled venison mixture with breadcrumbs, pepper flakes and cheese. Mix well, and season to taste with salt and pepper.

4. Divide mixture evenly into 4 parts. Each portion should stuff 4 mushroom caps (with some left over). Spoon mixture into caps, and place on a lightly greased baking pan. Place in the preheated oven for 6 to 7 minutes or until cheese is melted.

Pepper Poppers

I've made a variation of this recipe with everything from leftover fish to boar sausage, and it never fails to impress. If your DNA has you predisposed to eating really hot stuff, try it with hotter peppers like habaneros. The recipe specifies cooked ground venison, but it also works well with slow-cooked, pulled meat from roasts. It's also a way to make good use of leftover cooked venison.

6 appetizer servings

INGREDIENTS

- 18 fresh jalapeño or small sweet peppers
- 1 cup cooked ground venison
- 2 green onions, minced
- 2 tablespoons fresh basil, chopped
- 1 garlic clove, minced
- 1 teaspoon lime zest, minced
- $2/3$ cup shredded jack cheese
- 4 ounces cream cheese, room temperature
- ¼ cup seasoned breadcrumbs
- pinch or two salt

1. Place peppers on a baking sheet in a preheated 375-degree oven for 10 minutes. Remove from oven, and allow to cool. This will soften the peppers and make them easier to work with before stuffing. Leave the oven on 375 degrees.

2. Using a sharp knife, make a slit in each pepper from stem to tip, and carefully scoop out seeds.

3. In a bowl, combine remaining ingredients. Stuff into peppers. Don't worry if the peppers split a little. They will "seal" up when baking. Place on the same baking sheet, split side up, and place in the preheated oven for 6 to 8 minutes. Allow the peppers to rest a few minutes after removing from the oven so that they will firm up before serving.

Herb, Wine and Peppercorn Marinated Appetizer with Sweet Mustard Sauce

The marinade will add flavor to well-trimmed venison. For tougher cuts, lightly pound chunks of meat with a mallet to make them more tender before cooking. As with any venison, the longer you cook it past medium-rare, the tougher it will be. The sweet mustard sauce is quick and delicious.

4 to 6 appetizer servings

INGREDIENTS

- 1 pound venison, trimmed of all silver skin and gristle
- salt and pepper
- ¼ cup dry red wine
- 1 tablespoon lemon juice
- 2 cloves garlic, minced
- 2 tablespoons fresh herbs — rosemary, oregano, basil, sage or whatever looks good
- 2 tablespoons peppercorns, crushed
- 4 tablespoons olive oil

SWEET MUSTARD SAUCE

- ½ cup Dijon mustard
- ½ cup red currant jelly
- 1 lemon, juice only
- 1 tablespoon chopped sage

1. Combine sweet mustard sauce ingredients in a bowl and set aside.

2. Season meat liberally with salt and pepper. In a bowl, whisk together red wine, lemon juice, garlic, herbs and peppercorns. While whisking, add 2 tablespoons of the olive oil in a thin stream to emulsify marinade. Marinate for at least 2 hours, up to 12 hours. Longer time in the marinade will enhance the flavor.

3. Remove meat from marinade, pat dry and re-season with additional salt and pepper. Heat remaining 2 tablespoons oil in a large skillet, or cook on a well-oiled grill over medium-high heat, and brown meat evenly on all sides to desired doneness, which, for me, is medium-rare, or about 130 degrees in the center of the meat. Remove meat from heat, and let it rest for a few minutes before slicing into medallions across the grain. Arrange on a plate, and serve with sauce on the side for dipping.

Peanut and Sesame Crusted Tenderloin

The crust is deceptive. It looks like a fairly ordinary coating, but it's actually loaded with the flavor of roasted peanuts and toasted sesame seeds. I prefer to use more tender cuts of venison like tenderloins, but hindquarter muscles work just as well, provided that you first tenderize them with a mallet or other tenderizing device. Buy your sesame seeds in the Asian or Hispanic section of your market. They're much cheaper there than in the spice section.

4 to 6 appetizer servings

INGREDIENTS

- 1 or 2 tenderloins, depending on the size of the animal
- 1½ cups dry roasted peanuts
- ⅔ cup toasted sesame seeds
- ½ teaspoon salt
- ¼ cup Dijon mustard
- 1 tablespoon sesame oil
- 2 tablespoons soy sauce
- peanut oil
- 1 teaspoon lime juice

PEANUT DIPPING SAUCE

- 1 tablespoon hoisin sauce
- 3 tablespoons soy sauce
- 1 tablespoon pickled ginger
- 1 clove garlic, peeled
- 1 lime, juice only
- 1 tablespoon Asian Chili Garlic Sauce (Sriracha)
- 1½ tablespoons peanut butter
- 3 tablespoons rice vinegar

1. In a food processor, combine peanuts, sesame seeds and salt. Transfer to wide plate. In a small bowl, combine mustard, sesame oil and soy sauce and blend well.

2. Add peanut dipping sauce ingredients to blender, and process until smooth.

3. Evenly coat meat with mustard mixture. Roll coated meat into peanut and sesame seed mixture, pressing down so that coating sticks to tenderloin.

4. Heat a thin layer of peanut oil over medium-high heat in a large skillet. Carefully add coated tenderloin, and lightly brown on one side. Flip over and brown the other side. Drizzle lime juice over meat, remove meat from pan, and let rest for a few minutes before slicing into ½-inch thick medallions with a sharp, thin-bladed knife. Arrange on a plate with dipping sauce on the side.

Kinda Spicy Oven Jerky

Most folks think that they can't make jerky unless they have a dehydrator or smoker. Not so. Any oven will work just fine. Although making jerky can be a tester for those who lack basic knife skills, it's well worth the savings when compared to store-bought jerky, and you can make it exactly the way you want it — salty, spicy, sweet, it's your call. Here's a basic recipe for making oven jerky. It should be used as an outline. Add other ingredients to create your own signature jerky. Some prefer to add liquid smoke for flavor. If you are so inclined, use it sparingly. A little liquid smoke goes a long way.

As long as you're making jerky, it's best to make a large batch. Package in freezer-safe zipper-lock bags or, better, vacuum-pack them for longer storage. When cooled and packaged, they can be stored in the freezer for a year or more.

INGREDIENTS

- 2 pounds trimmed venison
- 1 teaspoon coarse-ground black pepper
- 1 teaspoon chili powder
- 2 teaspoons garlic powder
- 2 teaspoons onion powder
- ¼ cup brown sugar
- ¼ cup soy sauce
- ⅓ cup Worcestershire sauce
- ¼ cup hot sauce
- pan spray

1. Slice venison across the grain into ¼-inch thick strips. For a chewier jerky, slice along the grain. Combine remaining ingredients in a large bowl, blend well, add sliced jerky and toss to coat evenly. Cover and refrigerate for 12 to 24 hours, turning occasionally.

2. Remove jerky, and shake off excess marinade. Place a wire rack on top of a baking sheet, and lightly coat rack with pan spray. Lay meat out flat on rack, and place in a 160-degree oven. Oven door should be cracked open about ¼ to ¾ inch to allow moisture to escape. If you oven does not have a catch that will keep it cracked open, place a small foil ball between the door and the oven.

3. Flip meat over after about three hours. Place back in the oven, and continue drying. Making jerky isn't an exact science, although there are those who try to make it one. Check the meat again in another 3 hours. Remove the pieces that are thoroughly dried, and continue drying those that are not. Note that the meat should still be a little flexible and not crispy. It will firm up when cooled.

Savory Sliders

Miniature ground venison burgers loaded with fresh herbs, tomato and cheese are a great starter to keep hunger at bay while the main course is on the way. In a pinch, you can substitute 2 tablespoons of dried herbs or an herb blend (like Italian seasoning) in place of the fresh herbs. Load up a tray, and bring them to your next wild game potluck.

12 sliders

INGREDIENTS

- 1½ pounds ground venison, about 4½ cups
- 3 tablespoons flour
- ½ teaspoon salt
- ¼ teaspoon pepper
- 1 tablespoon garlic powder
- 1 cup canned diced tomato
- 2 tablespoons balsamic vinegar
- ⅓ cup fresh herbs, chopped — sage, rosemary, basil, parsley, whatever is available
- 12 small slices Swiss cheese
- small slider buns or Hawaiian sweet rolls

1. Combine flour, salt, pepper and garlic powder, and sprinkle evenly over meat. Work into meat to distribute evenly. This will help bind the meat together when cooked.

2. Place meat in a large bowl, and add remaining ingredients except cheese. Using your hands, mix thoroughly. Divide mixture into 3 equal portions. Divide each portion into 4 equal portions to make 12 patties. When forming burger patties, press firmly to help keep burgers intact while cooking.

3. Place on a medium-hot grill, griddle or skillet, and brown on one side. Flip over, cook for a couple of minutes more. Top with cheese, and cook until melted. Place in buns, and serve with condiments, if desired.

Crispy Spring Rolls

There isn't what you might call a "basic" spring roll. Some are fried, some are wrapped in softened rice paper, and the filling varies considerably. Here's a recipe for a crispy appetizer that's an unconventional use for venison, but it sure is good. Try it on your friends who long ago decided that they just don't like the taste of deer. It just might change their minds.

4 appetizer servings

INGREDIENTS

- 1½ cups venison from backstrap, tenderloin or hindquarter, trimmed
- 2 tablespoons soy sauce
- 1 teaspoon fresh ginger, minced
- 2 garlic cloves, minced
- 2 tablespoons peanut oil
- ¼ cup dried apricots, thinly sliced
- 1 cup cabbage, shredded
- 3 tablespoons fresh cilantro leaves, minced
- 8 egg roll wrappers
- 1 tablespoon cornstarch mixed with 1 tablespoon cold water
- oil for frying

DIPPING SAUCE

- ¼ cup soy sauce
- 1 tablespoon hoisin sauce (Asian section of your grocery store. It's there — really)
- 1 tablespoon brown sugar
- 2 tablespoons rice vinegar or white wine vinegar

1. Whisk together dipping sauce ingredients in a small bowl.

2. Slice venison as thinly as possible into 2- to 3-inch strips. Combine sliced venison with next three ingredients, and marinate for 1 hour. Remove meat from marinade and drain. Stir-fry meat in hot peanut oil for 45 to 60 seconds over high heat in a wok or skillet. Transfer to paper towels to cool.

3. In a small bowl, combine apricots, cabbage and cilantro. For each spring roll, lay the wrapper on a flat surface, and place about 2 to 3 tablespoons of the cabbage mixture on the lower third of the wrapper, forming an area of about 1 inch tall by 3 inches wide. Arrange cooked meat on top of cabbage. Turn in sides of wrapper to just overlap stuffing. Begin rolling egg roll by starting at the edge nearest you and rolling away from you, like a burrito. When you get to the edge, moisten it with a little of the cornstarch mixture to seal the edges like glue.

4. Heat 3 to 4 inches of oil in a heavy pot over medium-high heat. When hot, carefully add spring rolls, one or two at a time, into the oil, and fry until golden brown. Drain fried rolls on paper towels. Arrange on a plate, and serve with dipping sauce on the side.

Fried Ravioli

Making ravioli pasta is a relatively simple task, but I've come to the realization that very few people will take the time to do it. Store-bought wonton or egg roll wrappers are a little thinner than homemade, but they save time. It's best to keep a moist towel over the raw wraps to keep them from drying out.

24 ravioli

INGREDIENTS

FILLING

- 1 tablespoon vegetable oil
- ½ pound ground venison
- ¼ cup onion, minced
- 2 cloves garlic, minced
- ¼ cup fresh basil, minced
- 3 tablespoons Parmesan cheese, grated
- 1 egg, lightly beaten
- pinch salt
- pinch red chili flakes

- 48 wonton wrappers
- 2 tablespoons cornstarch
- 2 tablespoons cold water
- flour
- 1 cup buttermilk
- 2 cups breadcrumbs
- oil for frying
- 2 tablespoons dry mustard
- 2 tablespoons cold water
- ⅓ cup ketchup

1. Heat oil in a small skillet over medium heat. Add venison, onion and garlic, and lightly brown meat. Allow meat to cool, then add to a bowl with basil, cheese, egg, salt and chili flakes and mix well.

2. To keep wonton wrappers moist and pliable, prepare raviolis in 4 batches of 6 each. Place 6 wrappers on a flat surface. Place a quarter-sized ball of filling in the center of each. Stir together cornstarch and cold water, and spread a thin layer around the edges of each. That is the "glue" that holds the raviolis together. Place another wonton wrapper on the top of the filling, and press the edges of both wrappers together. Press as close to the filling as possible to minimize air space within the raviolis. Dust a work surface or tray with flour, and place the raviolis on the flour (to keep them from sticking to a surface or other raviolis). Repeat the process for the next 3 batches.

3. Place buttermilk and bread crumbs in separate bowls. Heat oil for frying in a heavy pot over medium-high heat. When oil is hot, dredge raviolis, one at a time, in buttermilk, then breadcrumbs, and carefully place in oil. Fry until golden brown. Drain on paper towels.

4. Arrange raviolis on a plate or platter. Stir mustard and cold water together. Place ketchup in a shallow bowl. Spoon mustard mixture onto the center of the ketchup. Raviolis can be dipped into the ketchup/mustard mixture. More mustard equals hotter sauce.

Tamales

Contrary to what some people believe, tamales do not come in a can. Yes, the label on the cans reads "tamales," but the difference between canned tamales and those made by hand is much like that of canned shrimp versus genuine Louisiana trawler-harvested shrimp. They're shrimp by name, but that's about the only similarity.

Getting the kitchen area set up for tamale production is a bit time-consuming. It's best done with a few people who each have a task. With everyone on board, making tamales goes quickly. And as long as the kitchen is set up to make tamales, make a big pile of them. They can be steamed, cooled, packaged and frozen for future consumption. Don't let the length of this recipe scare you off. The process is actually simple, but a little explanation in the beginning will make production easier.

THE MASA (THE DOUGH)

To prepare the masa, pick up a bag at the grocery store, and follow the directions on the bag for tamale dough. I start with 2 cups masa harina flour, ⅔ cup melted shortening, 1¼ cups warm chicken broth and ½ teaspoon salt. Start mixing with a fork, but eventually you'll need to get in there with your hands to make sure it's thoroughly mixed. The masa should be the consistency of moist cookie dough. If it's too dry, add a little more chicken broth. Too wet, mix in a little more masa harina flour.

THE CORN HUSKS

Dried corn husks are available in grocery stores and Hispanic markets. If you can't find them in yours, try it with fresh corn husks or parchment paper cut into a large triangle about the size of an outside corn husk.

THE STUFFING

Tamales can be stuffed with any cooked deer meat — ground, shredded or cubed. It should be tender to the bite before stuffing, or the cooked tamales will be chewy. Tougher cuts need to be simmered or braised until soft before adding to the stuffing.

Makes about 16 small tamales

INGREDIENTS

- 2 tablespoons vegetable oil
- ⅓ cup onion, diced
- 1 cup fresh tomatillos, quartered (or substitute green tomatoes or omit)
- 2 cloves garlic, minced
- 1 jalapeño pepper, seeded and minced
- 1 teaspoon chile powder
- ½ teaspoon ground cumin
- ¼ teaspoon salt
- 2 cups cooked venison, shredded or ground
- 3 cups masa (see Page 36)
- 16 corn husks, soaked in water for at least 1 hour
- large pot with lid and steamer basket or perforated insert

1. In a large skillet, heat oil over medium heat. Add onion, tomatillos, garlic and jalapeño and sauté for 3 to 4 minutes. Add chile powder, cumin, salt and cooked venison, and stir to blend flavors. Simmer for 2 to 3 minutes, and then allow to cool.

2. For each tamale, lay the corn husk on a flat surface with the narrow end pointing toward you. Take about 2 to 3 tablespoons of the masa, and spread evenly along the bottom quarter of the corn husk, about ½ inch from any edge of the husk. In the center of the masa, place a few tablespoons of the stuffing mixture. Fold the left edge over the stuffing. The idea is to surround the stuffing with masa. Fold the right edge over, and fold the bottom up toward the center.

3. Place in a hot steamer basket with the water level just under the bottom of the basket. Place tamales fold-side-down in basket, leaving a little room between each so that steam can cook each one. As they steam, check to make sure there is at least an inch or so of water in the pot. Tamales will take 25 to 40 minutes to steam, depending on how big they are. They will be soft, moist and hot when cooked and will firm up as they start to cool.

Garlic and Mustard Skewers

If garlic's not your thing, tone down the hot edge by first sautéing the cloves in olive oil over low heat until they are an even, light brown color. The flavor will be nutty and a little sweet.

6 appetizer servings

INGREDIENTS

- 1½ pounds venison, trimmed of any silver skin
- ¼ cup extra virgin olive oil
- 10 to 12 cloves fresh garlic, minced
- 2 tablespoons Worcestershire sauce
- 3 tablespoons soy sauce
- 1 tablespoon lemon juice
- 3 tablespoons Dijon mustard
- 1 tablespoon freshly ground black pepper
- ½ teaspoon kosher salt
- wooden skewers soaked in water for 30 minutes

1. Slice venison across the grain of the meat into ½-inch-thick strips.

2. In a medium bowl, whisk together remaining ingredients (except skewers). Add sliced meat to bowl, toss to coat evenly, cover and refrigerate for 1 to 4 hours, turning occasionally.

3. Remove meat from marinade and drain, but do not pat dry. Place skewers into meat, and grill to desired doneness over a well-oiled, medium-hot grill. For medium-rare, cooking time is about 3 to 4 minutes.

Tropical Quesadilla

OK, so maybe "tropical" is a bit clichéd, but there's more than just meat, cheese and flour tortillas in this tasty snack. The recipe calls for mango, but feel free to substitute fresh pineapple, papaya or, in a pinch, peaches or nectarines. The idea is to give it a sweet contrast to the spicy jalapeño pepper.

Makes 2 large quesadillas, 4 to 6 servings

INGREDIENTS

- 4 large ("burrito-sized") flour tortillas
- 2 cups pepper jack cheese, shredded
- 1½ cups cooked ground or shredded venison
- 1½ cups mango, peeled, seeded and diced
- ¼ cup red onion, finely diced
- ¼ cup jalapeño pepper, seeded and finely diced
- 1 teaspoon freshly squeezed lime juice
- 2 tablespoons cilantro leaves, minced
- 1½ cups cooked ground or shredded venison

1. In a medium bowl, combine mango, red onion, diced jalapeño, lime juice and cilantro.

2. Place 1 tortilla in a large skillet over medium heat. Spread ½ cup cheese evenly over tortilla. Add ¼ cup mango mixture and then cooked deer meat evenly across cheese. Top with another ½ cup cheese. Place another flour tortilla on top.

3. When lightly browned on one side, flip the quesadilla over to brown the other side. The easiest way is to place a dinner-sized plate, bottom side up, on top of the quesadilla while it is in the pan. Hold the bottom of the plate, grab the handle of the skillet with the other, and flip the quesadilla onto the plate. Then slide the quesadilla, browned side up, into the skillet. When browning the second side, press down gently to seal the quesadilla with the melted cheese.

4. Remove from pan, allow to cool for a few minutes. Cooling will also allow the quesadilla to firm up and hold together better when served. Slice into wedges, and arrange on a plate or platter.

chapter 3

Salads & Side Dishes

Growing up, I thought venison could only be cooked one way — slowly. Stews and slow-cookers were the rule unless the meat was ground into burgers or perhaps a meatloaf. Things have changed, at least for me, during the past few decades. Venison has broken out of the main-dish mold and found its way into any place on the menu you can find beef, lamb or pork.

Before adding cooked venison meat to a side dish, give it a few minutes to "rest" so the juices redistribute within the meat and don't run out onto an otherwise pristine salad or other side dish. This section includes a recipe or two for making your own salad dressings or seasonings. If you have favorite store-bought varieties that will work just as well, use them and save some time in the kitchen. All of the side dishes and salads can be adjusted to make main-course or first-course servings.

Grilled Thai Salad

Contrary to what some folks think, Thai cuisine is not just fiery heat and oddball ingredients. It's fresh, light and long on flavor. Because you're making your own, add more or fewer red pepper flakes to suit your taste buds.

4 servings

INGREDIENTS

- 1 pound venison backstrap, tenderloin or trimmed hindquarter steak
- ½ cup olive oil
- ¼ cup Asian fish sauce
- 1½ tablespoons sugar
- ⅓ cup freshly squeezed lemon juice
- 3 cloves garlic, minced
- ⅓ cup fresh mint leaves, minced
- ½ teaspoon red pepper flakes

- ¼ teaspoon freshly ground black pepper
- 2 heads red leaf lettuce, outside leaves removed; torn into large pieces
- 1 head romaine lettuce heart, roughly chopped
- 4 radishes, rinsed and thinly sliced
- 1 cup cilantro leaves, loosely packed
- ½ red onion, thinly sliced

1. Rub venison with 1 tablespoon olive oil. Heat a large skillet over medium-high heat, and brown meat evenly on both sides, but not past medium-rare. Allow to cool, and then slice diagonally into thin strips. Place in a medium bowl.

2. Prepare dressing. In a medium bowl, whisk together fish sauce, sugar, lemon juice, garlic, mint, red pepper flakes and black pepper. While whisking, add remaining oil in a thin stream until emulsified. Pour ½ of the dressing mixture over sliced and cooled venison, and toss to coat. Refrigerate for 1 hour.

3. In a large bowl, toss together lettuce, radishes, cilantro and red onion. Drizzle reserved dressing over, and lightly toss again. Mound lettuce mixture on plates, and top with marinated venison.

Sausage and White Beans

This is a stick-to-your ribs side dish that can also be served as a main course. If I'm short on time, I'll make a quick version of this recipe with 4 15-ounce cans of cooked beans instead of dried. Any venison sausage will do, but my sausage of choice for this dish is Italian-seasoned.

8 side dish servings

INGREDIENTS

- Bean preparation
- 1 pound dried cannellini beans
- 3 tablespoons olive oil
- 3 quarts chicken broth
- 3 cloves garlic, minced
- 2 cups onion, diced
- 2 cups celery, diced
- 2 bay leaves
- 6 black peppercorns, crushed

- 3 tablespoons olive oil
- 2 pounds venison sausage, diced
- 3 cloves garlic, minced
- 1 15-ounce can plum tomatoes, chopped
- 1 cup tomato puree
- 2 tablespoons red wine vinegar
- 1 teaspoon sugar
- salt and pepper
- 1/3 cup Italian parsley, chopped

1. Place beans in a large pot, and cover with 2½ quarts water. Bring water to a boil, and cook beans, uncovered, over moderate heat 2 minutes. Remove pan from heat, and soak beans for 1 hour.

2. Drain the beans, and return to pot. Add olive oil, chicken broth, garlic, onion, celery, bay leaves and peppercorns, and bring to a boil. Cover, reduce heat to low, and simmer for two hours or until beans are tender.

3. Heat oil in a large skillet over medium heat. Add venison sausage, and brown evenly. Add 1 cup of the liquid from the beans, garlic, plum tomatoes, tomato puree, vinegar and sugar. Heat until thickened, about 5 minutes. Season to taste with salt and pepper.

4. Drain beans in a colander, and spoon a serving portion into bowls or serve family-style in a large bowl. Spoon sausage mixture over beans, and top with parsley.

Deer Fried Rice

Suppose you've got some leftover rice and maybe a cup or two of venison. You've probably tried pork fried rice, so why not deer fried rice? It's a great accompaniment for a wild game stir-fry. Next time you're in the market, see if you can find ponzu sauce in the Asian section. It has less sodium than low-sodium soy sauce and citrus juice. Better flavor, less salt.

4 servings

INGREDIENTS

- 1 tablespoon peanut oil
- ½ teaspoon sesame oil
- 4 green onions, chopped
- ½ cup carrots, finely diced
- 3 cloves garlic, minced
- ½ teaspoon ginger, peeled and minced
- 1 cup diced venison
- ¼ cup low-sodium soy sauce
- 1 teaspoon hoisin sauce
- 2 cups cooked white or brown rice
- 2 eggs, beaten
- salt and black pepper

1. Heat peanut and sesame oil in a large skillet or wok over medium heat. Add green onions, carrots, garlic and ginger, and stir-fry for 2 minutes. Add venison, and cook for 2 minutes more. Add soy sauce and hoisin sauce. Cook for 1 minute.

2. Add rice and egg, and stir-fry until hot throughout and egg is completely cooked. Season to taste with salt and pepper.

Stuffed Zucchini

I grew up eating this dish, prepared with ground beef, a few times a month. I've since made it many times with various ground game meats and game sausage. It might be pedestrian for today's food snobs, but it really tastes great.

4 servings

INGREDIENTS

- 2 medium zucchini, split lengthwise
- 1 tablespoon olive oil
- ½ pound ground venison
- ½ pound ground Italian sausage (or ground Italian venison sausage)
- ½ cup onion, diced
- ½ cup bell pepper, diced
- 2 garlic cloves, minced
- 1 cup tomato sauce
- 2 teaspoons Italian seasoning
- ½ cup breadcrumbs
- ½ teaspoon salt
- ¼ teaspoon black pepper
- 1½ cups mozzarella cheese

1. Preheat oven to 350 degrees. Using a spoon, scoop out the seed section of the zucchini. Save ¾ of the pulp, roughly chop and place in a medium bowl.

2. Heat oil in a large skillet over medium heat. Add venison and sausage. Cook until evenly browned. Add onion, pepper and garlic, and cook 3 to 4 minutes more. Transfer to bowl with zucchini pulp, and add tomato sauce, Italian seasoning, salt, pepper and half of the cheese. Mix well.

3. Place the zucchini, scooped side up, in a lightly greased baking dish. Spoon stuffing mixture into zucchini. Top with remaining cheese, and place in the preheated oven for 15 minutes, or until the cheese is lightly browned and bubbly.

Venison Carpaccio

I used to eat raw venison as part of my wild-game cooking demonstrations. To those who only ate antlered game cooked well-done or "all the way," it was like watching someone eat live insects. Even people who enjoy their venison rare or medium-rare would often blanch at the sight of me eating it raw. I urge you to give this taste of venison a try and to savor each tender bite. Note that it is neither gamey nor chewy. If your venison doesn't taste this good after you cook it, you shouldn't blame the deer.

4 to 6 servings

INGREDIENTS

- 1 venison backstrap — center section, about 6 to 8 inches long
- 1 cup fresh rosemary leaves, minced
- 2 tablespoons coarse ground black pepper
- 1 tablespoon kosher or sea salt
- 2 garlic cloves, minced
- ⅓ cup olive oil
- plastic wrap
- 4 cups spring mix lettuce
- ½ teaspoon Dijon mustard
- 2 teaspoons freshly squeezed lemon juice
- 1 tablespoon balsamic vinegar
- 2 tablespoons capers, rinsed
- 3 tablespoons red onion, minced
- ¼ teaspoon sugar
- ⅓ cup Parmesan cheese, shaved

1. Remove silver skin from backstrap. Combine rosemary, pepper, salt and garlic, and spread out on a cutting board or work surface. Roll trimmed backstrap in rosemary mixture, and press firmly while rolling.

2. Heat 2 tablespoons of the oil in a large skillet. Carefully add backstrap, and cook on all sides for about 1 minute per side. The goal is for the rosemary mixture to adhere to the backstrap. Allow to cool completely before wrapping tightly in plastic wrap. Place in the freezer for at least 3 hours or until completely frozen.

3. Whisk together remaining olive oil, mustard, lemon juice, vinegar, capers, red onion and sugar.

4. Before serving, remove backstrap from freezer, and let rest at room temperature for 30 minutes to soften somewhat, but it should still be frozen. Using a sharp, thin-bladed knife, slice into rounds as thinly as possible without shredding. Think "paper thin." Arrange slices in a wide circle on plates. Lettuce mix will be placed in the center.

5. In a bowl, toss lettuce in a few tablespoons of the dressing, saving about the same amount of dressing to drizzle over backstrap. Mound lettuce in the center of plates. Drizzle remaining dressing over meat. Top lettuce with Parmesan cheese.

Tostada

It's just a taco unhinged. This can be a salad or appetizer course, or double the recipe for a light lunch or dinner entrée.

4 servings

INGREDIENTS

- 4 cups cooked ground or pulled venison, seasoned with Southwestern seasonings
- 4 large corn tortillas, deep-fried until crispy
- 2 cups cooked black beans
- 6 cups romaine or iceberg lettuce, thinly chopped
- 8 thin slices red onion
- 2 cups pepper jack cheese, grated
- ½ cup chopped black olives
- 1½ cups red or green salsa
- ¼ cup sour cream

1. For each serving, place a tortilla on a plate. Top with ½ cup black beans, 1½ cups lettuce, 1 cup cooked venison, 2 slices red onion, ½ cup cheese, 2 tablespoons olives, salsa and a dollop of sour cream.

Gruyére and Ground Venison Baked Portabello Mushroom

Grilled earthy portabello mushrooms are filled with seasoned ground venison and topped with melted cheese. It just sounds good, doesn't it?

4 servings

INGREDIENTS

- 4 large portabello mushrooms
- 1 tablespoon olive oil
- 2 cloves garlic, minced
- 2 green onions, chopped
- 1 tablespoon fresh sage leaves, minced (or pinch or two dried sage)
- ¾ pound ground venison
- ½ cup tomato, seeded and diced
- salt and pepper
- 4 slices Gruyére cheese

1. Remove stems from mushrooms. With a spoon, scrape dark brown gills away from their undersides. Be careful around the edges of the mushroom caps so that they do not get torn or broken. If they get broken, it's no big deal. It will just be a little messier when served. Preheat oven to 400 degrees. Place mushrooms on a baking sheet, top side down, and roast for 6 to 7 minutes.

2. Heat oil in a skillet over medium heat. Add garlic, onions and sage, and cook 2 to 3 minutes. Add venison and cook until browned, about 4 to 5 minutes. Stir in tomato, and season to taste with salt and pepper.

3. Spoon equal portions of the venison mixture into mushrooms. Place a slice of cheese on top of each. Return to oven, and roast until cheese is melted and lightly browned.

Iceberg Wedge with Crispy Venison

Lots of people knock iceberg lettuce for its lack of nutritional value as compared to other lettuces. Iceberg is low on vitamins A and C compared to darker-leafed greens, but it's crisp, crunchy and sits high and proud on a plate. This recipe simply builds a classic wedge-and-blue-cheese salad upon seasoned, pounded and seared venison medallions. If desired, substitute your favorite brand of prepared blue cheese dressing for the recipe below.

4 large servings

INGREDIENTS

- 1 pound venison from backstrap or hindquarter, trimmed
- salt and pepper
- 3 tablespoons vegetable oil
- 1 large tomato, cut into 4 equal slices
- 1 head iceberg lettuce, outer leaves removed —
  cut into 4 wedges from stem end to top
- 1 red onion, thinly sliced and broken into rings
- 1 firm, ripe avocado — peeled, seeded and quartered
- $1/3$ cup cooked bacon, crumbled
- ¼ cup blue cheese, crumbled

DRESSING

- ¼ pound crumbled blue cheese
- 2 tablespoons sour cream
- 3 tablespoons buttermilk
- ¼ cup mayonnaise
- 2 tablespoons red wine vinegar
- 2 teaspoons olive oil
- 2 teaspoons white sugar
- 1 clove garlic, minced
- ground black pepper to taste

1. To prepare dressing, combine all ingredients in a blender or food processor, and pulse until smooth. Keep refrigerated until ready to dress salad.

2. Cut venison into 4 equal portions. Season liberally with salt and pepper. Place between plastic wrap, and lightly pound until very thin. If the meat tears a little while pounding, it's OK. It needs to be thin enough to be very tender when cooked. Heat vegetable oil in a large skillet over high heat. Add venison, 1 or 2 pieces at a time, and cook for about 2 minutes per side or until well browned and crisp. Allow cooked meat to rest for a few minutes before placing flat on the center of each plate.

3. For each salad, place a tomato slice on the center of the venison. Place a wedge on top of the lettuce. Arrange a few onion rings around lettuce. Place an avocado wedge at the base of the lettuce. Drizzle dressing over lettuce. Top with bacon and crumbled blue cheese. If desired, grind additional pepper over salad.

Grilled Fajita-Style Salad

Assertive Southwestern flavors make this main dish salad a palate pleaser for those who like it well-seasoned but not too spicy hot. I like to serve this with warm flour tortillas and cold Mexican beer.

4 large servings

INGREDIENTS

THE MEAT

- 1 pound venison tenderloin, backstrap or tenderized hindquarter steak
- 1 cup bell pepper, 2 or 3 colored peppers, if available — seeded and thinly sliced
- 1 large yellow onion, thinly sliced
- 3 cloves garlic, minced
- 2 tablespoons freshly squeezed lime juice
- 2 tablespoons olive oil

THE SEASONING

(or use your favorite prepared Southwestern seasoning blend)

- ½ teaspoon garlic powder
- ½ teaspoon cayenne pepper
- ¼ teaspoon cumin
- ¼ teaspoon oregano
- 1 teaspoon paprika
- ½ teaspoon salt
- 1 teaspoon chili powder
- 1 teaspoon sugar

THE SALAD

- 1 tablespoon cider vinegar
- 2 tablespoons freshly squeezed lime juice
- 1 teaspoon Dijon mustard
- 1 tablespoon agave nectar (or honey)
- ¼ cup fresh cilantro leaves
- ½ cup olive oil
- salt and pepper
- 2 heads romaine lettuce, outside leaves removed — roughly chopped
- 1 avocado, peeled, seeded and cut into cubes
- 1½ cups tomato, chopped

1. Combine seasoning ingredients (or use your own seasoning blend).

2. Slice venison across the grain into ¼-inch thick strips. Toss with seasoning. Combine sliced meat with other meat ingredients in a non-reactive bowl or zipper lock bag, and refrigerate for 2 to 3 hours.

3. Prepare dressing. In a blender or food processor, combine cider vinegar with next 5 ingredients. Process until dressing is smooth. Season to taste with salt and pepper.

4. Remove meat ingredients from refrigerator, and let stand at room temperature for 30 minutes. Heat a large skillet over medium-high heat. Add meat ingredients, and stir-fry until meat is just cooked, about 5 to 7 minutes.

5. While meat is cooking, toss lettuce, avocado and tomato with dressing in a large bowl. Mound salad mix on plates. Spoon cooked meat mixture over center of salad mix.

Blackened Backstrap Salad with Romaine, Dried Cranberries and Feta

A home version of a popular chop house salad — spicy seared choice cut of venison paired with crisp lettuce, mild feta cheese and an occasional bite of a sweet cranberry. You can make your own blackening spices with a mixture of white, black and cayenne peppers, along with salt and any additional savory spices that make you happy, but store-bought blends are just fine. Blackening of meats occurs when the spices on the outside are burnt. Contrary to what you might have heard elsewhere, searing meat on the outside doesn't "seal in the juices," but it sure makes it taste better.

4 large servings

INGREDIENTS

- 1 pound venison backstrap
- 2 tablespoons olive oil
- 2 tablespoons blackening spices
- 2 heads Romaine lettuce, outer leaves removed — roughly chopped
- 1 cup dried cranberries
- 1 large slice red onion
- 1 small cucumber, peeled and thinly sliced
- 4 medium tomatoes, cut into wedges
- 1 cup crumbled feta cheese

DRESSING

- ¼ cup balsamic vinegar
- 1 teaspoon lemon juice
- ½ teaspoon Dijon mustard
- 1 teaspoon sugar

- 2 garlic cloves, minced
- ½ teaspoon salt
- ½ teaspoon pepper
- ¾ cup olive oil

1. Rub backstrap with olive oil. Coat with blackening spices, wrap with plastic wrap, and refrigerate for 2 to 3 hours. Remove from refrigerator, and let rest at room temperature for 20 minutes. While meat is resting, heat a heavy duty (preferably cast iron) skillet over high heat until it is very hot. "Smoking hot" is best, but make sure that you open a window or two for ventilation. Add meat to pan, and blacken on all sides, keeping the center of the meat as close to medium-rare as possible. Remove meat, and let it rest.

2. Prepare dressing. In a bowl, whisk together all dressing ingredients except olive oil. While whisking, add olive oil in a thin stream until emulsified.

3. In a large bowl, toss lettuce and cranberries with a light coating of dressing. Mound lettuce mix on plates. Arrange onion, cucumber and tomato around lettuce.

4. Thinly slice backstrap across the grain, and arrange on top of lettuce. Drizzle additional dressing over meat, and top with feta cheese.

Warning: Burning pepper in a hot skillet has the same effect as breathing in pepper spray. Turn on the fan, open up the doors and windows, and do not breathe in the fumes directly above the pan.

Venison Sausage, Bacon, Mushrooms and Spinach

This is a quickie that is best made just before serving so the spinach isn't completely wilted.

4 servings

INGREDIENTS

- 4 strips bacon, diced
- 2 cups venison sausage, thinly sliced (or crumbled, if sausage is ground, not linked)
- 1 red bell pepper, seeded and sliced into thin strips
- 2 cups mushrooms, thinly sliced
- 1 teaspoon lemon juice
- 3 tablespoons rice vinegar
- 1 tablespoon Dijon mustard
- pinch of sugar
- ½ teaspoon coarse ground pepper
- 4 big handfuls fresh spinach, stems removed
- salt
- shaved Parmesan cheese

1. Brown bacon in a large skillet over medium heat. Add venison, and brown evenly. Add bell pepper and mushrooms, and cook for 2 minutes. Stir in lemon juice, vinegar, mustard, sugar and pepper. Heat for 1 minute more.

2. Add spinach to pan, and cook until spinach just starts to wilt. Season with salt to taste. Mound on plates and top with cheese.

Marinated Ravioli with Lemon Vinaigrette

Served warm, chilled or room temperature, this is a fitting side dish for any season.

4 servings

INGREDIENTS

- 24 venison ravioli ("Small Bites" — "Fried Ravioli," Page 34)

LEMON VINAIGRETTE

- 1 tablespoon lemon zest
- 2 tablespoons freshly squeezed lemon juice
- 1 tablespoon white wine vinegar
- ¾ teaspoon Dijon mustard
- 1 teaspoon honey
- 2 tablespoons fresh Italian parsley leaves, minced
- ½ cup olive oil
- 2 cloves garlic, minced
- ½ cup tomato, seeded and diced
- salt and pepper

1. Prepare vinaigrette. In a bowl, whisk together lemon zest and next 5 ingredients. While whisking, add olive oil in a thin stream until emulsified. Stir in garlic and tomato. Season to taste with salt and pepper.

2. Heat 3 quarts of water over medium heat. When water just starts to boil, add ravioli, a few at a time, and cook for 2 to 3 minutes. Carefully remove ravioli with a slotted spoon, and drain in a colander, but do not rinse. Transfer to a shallow bowl and immediately toss gently with vinaigrette. Can be served immediately, left to rest until room temperature or chilled in the refrigerator for an hour or two.

Warm Venison and Mushroom Salad

Mushrooms and venison are a great match, especially if you know your way around the woods and can forage, rather than shop, for local shrooms. High-dollar mushrooms such as morels and chanterelles can be gathered by the buckets in some parts of the country, but it's critically important that you can tell the difference between the edibles and the ones that will make you really sick. When in doubt, don't eat them. I use trimmed venison backstrap, tenderloin or hindquarter muscles for this dish.

4 servings

INGREDIENTS

- ½ cup pecan pieces
- 1 tablespoon olive oil
- ½ teaspoon kosher salt
- dash or two Tabasco
- 1½ cups cooked (rare to medium-rare) venison, thinly sliced
- ⅓ cup olive oil
- 4 cups mushrooms, thinly sliced
- 2 garlic cloves, minced

- 3 lemons, juice only
- ¼ cup fresh basil, chopped
- ½ teaspoon Dijon mustard
- 4 handfuls arugula
- ⅓ cup Gorgonzola cheese, crumbled
- ½ red onion, thinly sliced
- 1 cup diced tomato

1. Toss pecans with 1 tablespoon olive oil, kosher salt and Tabasco. Place on a baking sheet, and place sheet in a preheated 325-degree oven. Toast pecans until darker brown, but not burnt. Remove from oven and cool.

2. Heat ⅓ cup olive oil in a skillet over medium-high heat. Add mushrooms and garlic and sauté for 3 to 4 minutes. Mushrooms should still be a little firm. Stir in basil, mustard and sliced cooked venison. Heat to warm, and blend ingredients.

3. For each serving, mound arugula on plates. Spoon mushroom and venison mixture over. Top with cheese, onion and tomato. Drizzle any remaining dressing over.

Venison Rarebit

I first had the non-meat, traditional version of this recipe when I was about 6 years old, while dining with my family at Chowning's Tavern in Williamsburg, Va. There's some history behind it that dates back to 18th century Great Britain. The classic dish, Welsh rarebit, is basically a hot, cheesy sauce spooned over cheesy bread. For years, I thought it was called Welsh rabbit, not rarebit, made with real rabbit. The word "rarebit" supposedly is a corruption of an original dish that might have included rabbit. I'm not too concerned where the word originated, just how the dish tastes. This dish can also be made with slow-cooked pulled venison from the shoulder, neck or hindquarter. You will need 4 smallish baking dishes, or "boats," or prepare all four servings together in one large baking dish.

4 servings

INGREDIENTS

THE RAREBIT

- 1 pound cheddar cheese
- 6 ounces whole milk
- 3 ounces flat ale
- salt, pepper and cayenne pepper to taste
- ½ teaspoon coarse-grained mustard
- 4 thick slices of French or sourdough bread, toasted
- 4 lightly buttered small baking dishes

THE VENISON

- 1 pound venison steak, trimmed
- 3 tablespoons olive oil
- salt and pepper

1. Preheat oven to 350 degrees. Rub venison liberally with olive oil, salt and pepper. Grill or pan sear over medium-high heat until just cooked. Let cool before slicing into small cubes.

2. Melt cheese in the top of a double boiler. Add milk and beer a little at a time while stirring, until sauce is smooth. Season to taste with salt, pepper and cayenne. Stir in mustard. To serve, place toast in buttered baking dishes. Top with cooked venison, and top with cheese sauce.

3. Place baking dishes on a baking pan, and place in the preheated oven for 15 minutes and serve.

chapter 4
Soups & Stews

It seems like you can't just say "soups" without saying "stews." One's a little thinner, and the other's more of a hardy, stick-to-your-ribs type of main-course dish. Both are delicious and great ways to make the best use of venison parts that are most often discarded. Roasted venison and rosemary stock sure sounds better than beef bouillon cubes, doesn't it?

What is "Stew Meat?"

Meaty soup and stew recipes often call for something called stew meat. Because I'm not aware of a specific animal body part that's called a stew, the term could use some clarification, at least as it pertains to this cookbook. Stewing a backstrap or tenderloin is a terrible waste of the tenderest parts of a deer. Part of the beauty of soups and stews is that the simmering process turns otherwise tough cuts of venison into super tender morsels. When simmered in liquid, pretty much any cut of venison will eventually get tender. If it's not tender to the touch, keep cooking. It'll get there. Stew meat can be any chunk of meat, usually cut into 1- to 3-inch pieces. If you process your own animals, save any bits of meat trimmed from the entire animal. Package properly, label and store in the freezer.

Venison Stock or Broth

Soups and stews start with some form of liquid, usually made from a mix of meat and vegetables. The liquid imparts flavor, breaks down fibrous muscles and joins flavors for a bowl full of something warm and comforting. It seems a shame to start your concoction with salty bouillon cubes or granules. There really is no flavor comparison between homemade stock and the foil-wrapped cube. The only upside to the cube is convenience. It's been my experience that you'll rarely find something good to eat at a convenience store.

Bones, joints and skin contain collagen, giving a stock its depth of flavor. By the way, most home chefs are confused about the distinction between a stock and a broth. Don't let it concern you. Basically, a broth is a more seasoned, refined version of a stock, which is fairly bland until you add a pinch or two of salt. For the foodies, yes, I know the differences between the two run a little deeper. For most of us cooking types, it really doesn't matter what you call it, and I've used stocks and broths interchangeably. The important thing to remember is to hoard, not discard, your game bones, shanks and carcasses. Save them for the stock pot.

A proper homemade stock will always taste better than something you buy from the store. They get their rich, deep flavor from roasted bones and vegetables. Although stocks are traditionally made with roasting marrow bones, I'll also throw meaty animal parts into the roasting pan when making them. My freezer is loaded with meat scraps, carcasses and bones. When I run out of room, it's time to make stocks and broths.

My family can always tell when it's a "stock day." The telltale signs are steamy windows, tall pots on the stove and the unmistakable aroma of simmering roasted meat and vegetables. I'm not sure that my wife fully appreciates the advantages of a homemade stock. The smell of game stock tends to hang around for a while. Oh sure, the shutters get a little greasy, and the stovetop's a mess, but it's worth it. It's always best to schedule a kitchen cleaning day after you make stocks.

When the stocks are prepared, they can be frozen. Strain and season the liquid. Then make it smaller. A gallon of stock reduced down to one quart will take up much less space in the freezer. Fill up ice-cube trays and, when frozen, dump them into a freezer-safe zipper lock bag. When a recipe calls for broth or stock, grab a cube and add three parts water for about one cup of liquid. You can also freeze flat in the same zipper-lock bags, and break off a corner or two when needed. As with any frozen protein, mark the bag with the date and specific type of stock or broth.

Venison Stock

The measurements aren't really exact. Basically, you brown it, simmer it, strain it and reduce it. This recipe includes red wine, but it's only a personal preference. Substitute water for wine, if desired. When you taste the finished stock, you'll notice that it is somewhat bland. Seasoned with a pinch of salt and pepper, it will come to life.

About 1 gallon stock

INGREDIENTS

- 5 to 6 pounds venison marrow bones, sawed or cracked into 3- to 4-inch pieces
- venison scraps, if available — up to 3 pounds
- 2 large carrots, chopped
- 3 celery stalks, chopped
- 1 yellow onion, chopped
- 6 garlic cloves
- olive oil (optional)
- cheap red wine
- cold water
- 1 tablespoon black peppercorns
- bouquet garni (a bunch of herbs tied together with string)
- salt

1. Preheat oven to 400 degrees. Place venison bones and scraps in a large roasting pan. Add carrot, celery, onion and garlic. To aid in browning, drizzle a thin stream of olive oil over, and toss to coat. Place in oven for 1½ hours, turning contents every 20 minutes, until evenly browned. When browned, stir 1 cup wine into the pan and roast for another 15 minutes.

2. Transfer contents of the pan to a large stock pot, scraping the bottom of the pan to loosen bits. Pour 2 cups of red wine into stock pot and enough water to just cover contents of the pot. Add peppercorns and bouquet garni. Simmer, uncovered over low heat for 6 to 8 hours, making sure that you keep enough liquid in the pot to just cover contents.

3. Pour contents through a colander covered with cheesecloth or paper towels. Discard contents of colander (or feed meat to dogs). Transfer liquid (stock) to a medium stock pot. Season to taste with salt, and simmer until liquid is reduced by at least ½. Cool and skim off any fat from the top before storage.

Deer and Barley Soup

This recipe calls for onions, carrots and celery, but you can use any vegetables you have on hand. If you can't find barley, use rice, pasta or potatoes. I like to serve it with homemade croutons topped with some melted Parmesan or jack cheese.

6 to 8 servings

INGREDIENTS

- 2 pounds venison stew meat, trimmed and cut into 1-inch cubes
- salt and pepper
- 2 tablespoons vegetable oil
- 1 large onion, diced
- 4 stalks celery, diced
- 3 carrots, diced
- 4 garlic cloves, minced
- 2 quarts game broth or beef broth
- 2 sprigs fresh rosemary (optional)
- 3 cups cooked barley (prepare as per package)

1. Season meat liberally with salt and pepper. Heat oil in a large stock pot over medium-high heat, add meat and brown evenly. Add onion, celery, carrots and garlic. Cook 5 minutes or until onions are translucent. Add broth and rosemary. Bring to a boil, then reduce heat to low, and simmer until meat is soft and tender.

2. Remove rosemary and stir in barley. Serve with warm bread or croutons.

Sweet Potato Stew

The first few times I made this stew, it was based on a Moroccan recipe with prominent curry, turmeric and cinnamon flavors. Turns out that I don't really care much for curry, turmeric and cinnamon, so the recipe eventually transitioned into the one below, resembling more of a traditional stew. If you like the aforementioned spices, add a pinch or two of each, and eat like a Moroccan.

6 to 8 servings

INGREDIENTS

- 3 cups venison stew meat, cut into 1-inch pieces
- ¾ cup flour, seasoned with 2 teaspoons salt and 1 teaspoon pepper
- ¼ cup vegetable oil
- ½ cup dry red wine
- 1½ cups onion, diced
- 2 cups carrots, peeled and diced
- 1 cup bell pepper, diced
- 4 cloves garlic, minced
- 1½ quarts beef or venison stock
- 1 bay leaf
- ¼ cup tomato paste
- 2 cups sweet potatoes, peeled and diced into 1-inch chunks
- 1 tablespoon fresh thyme leaves, minced (or substitute ¾ teaspoon dried thyme)
- 1 tablespoon sugar
- salt and pepper
- 6 cups warm cooked couscous
- chopped parsley for garnish

1. In a large bowl, toss venison, flour, salt and pepper, and coat evenly. Heat 3 tablespoons oil in a large pot over medium-high heat. Add venison, and brown evenly. Remove venison from pot, and set aside.

2. To the same pot, add wine and stir to deglaze pot. Add 2 more tablespoons oil and onion, carrots, bell pepper and garlic. Cook, while stirring occasionally, for 5 minutes. Return meat to the pot, add stock and bay leaf, and bring to a boil. Reduce heat to low and simmer, uncovered, for 45 to 60 minutes or until meat just starts to get tender.

3. Add tomato paste, sweet potatoes, thyme and sugar. Simmer for another 15 to 20 minutes. When sweet potatoes are just cooked, season to taste with salt and pepper.

4. To serve, spoon couscous into bowls, and ladle stew over. Sprinkle parsley over top.

Chile Colorado

There's always been some confusion regarding the various spellings of chili, er ... I mean chile. After consulting various resources, the majority suggest that chile is the pepper and chili is the dish. But then there's chile verde and chile Colorado, both dishes that end with an e, not i. I really don't care how it's spelled as long as it tastes good.

I'm guessing that most folks don't know what to do with those earthy dried red peppers they see hanging on the racks in the Hispanic section of the local market. Here's the deal — pull the stems off, scrape out the seeds, soak them in hot water for 30 minutes, and process them in a blender or food processor. It's the "red" in red chile and red enchilada sauce. The recipe specifies New Mexico dried chiles, but any large dried red chile will suffice.

This chile screams Southwestern flavor. Not in a bad, mouth-on-fire sort of way, but in a, "Wow, now that's one incredible chile (or chili)" way. You can't get this depth of flavor out of a can.

6 to 8 servings

INGREDIENTS

- 6 to 8 New Mexico dried chiles, washed and stems removed
- 2 pounds venison stew meat, cut into 1-inch cubes
- 1 large onion, chopped
- 2 Anaheim peppers, chopped
- 6 garlic cloves, finely minced
- 1 28-ounce can tomatoes, diced
- 2 7-ounce cans whole mild green (Anaheim or "Ortega" type) chiles, chopped
- ½ teaspoon dried oregano leaves
- 2 cups beef broth
- salt and pepper
- flour tortillas, warm
- shredded cheese
- salsa
- shredded lettuce

1. Place chiles in a small saucepan with 2½ cups water. Bring to a boil, remove from heat, and steep chiles for 30 minutes. Place softened chiles and about ½ cup of the liquid in a food processor or blender. Process until smooth, adding additional liquid if necessary to puree. Pass mixture through a strainer to remove seeds and any bits of skin.

2. Heat oil in a large saucepan over medium-high heat. Add meat and brown evenly. Add onion, peppers and garlic, and cook until onions are translucent.

3. Add tomatoes, canned chiles, oregano, beef broth and processed chiles. Cover and bring to a boil. Reduce heat to low, and simmer for 2 hours or until meat is tender. While cooking, make sure that there is always enough liquid to barely cover meat. Season to taste with salt and pepper.

4. To serve, ladle chile into bowls, and serve with warm flour tortillas, cheese, salsa and chopped onions on the side. Guests can spoon chile onto tortillas and add desired toppings.

Chile Verde

I've used this recipe with an assortment of game animals including elk, deer, feral hogs and waterfowl. Serve with warm flour tortillas, shredded lettuce, tomato, cheese, sour cream and cold Mexican beer.

6 to 8 servings

INGREDIENTS

- 3 pounds venison stew meat, cut into 1-inch pieces
- 3 tablespoons vegetable oil
- 2 quarts chicken broth
- 2 cups yellow onion, chopped
- 8 garlic cloves, chopped
- 2 green bell peppers, chopped
- 1 red bell pepper, chopped
- 2 Anaheim peppers, chopped
- 3 jalapeño peppers, seeded and diced
- 1 tablespoon dried oregano flakes
- 2 tablespoons chili powder
- 2 tablespoons ground cumin
- 1 teaspoon cayenne pepper
- 2 cups fresh tomatillos, skin removed; quartered (or canned/drained)
- 1 cup fresh cilantro leaves, chopped
- salt and pepper
- 2 limes, quartered

1. Heat oil in a large stock pot over medium-high heat. Add meat, and brown evenly. Drain off any fat or liquid rendered during browning. Add 1½ quart chicken broth and any additional broth or water to cover meat, and bring to a boil. Reduce heat and simmer, covered, for 2 hours or until meat is tender and breaks apart, but doesn't fall apart, with moderate finger pressure. Drain liquid from stock pot. Add remaining 2 cups of chicken stock and all other ingredients except cilantro. Simmer until peppers are tender. Stir in cilantro, and season with salt and pepper to taste.

2. Serve in bowls with limes on the side.

Grilled Venison, Tomato, Pepper and Corn Stew

This is a lighter stew I prepare during summer, when corn and tomatoes are in season and at the peak of flavor. Fire up the grill, sear the meat and vegetables, and simmer in a savory stock. Because this is a quicker than a normal version of a stew, use better cuts of venison. To remove seeds from tomatoes, cut widthwise in half, and place your fingers into the open halves, removing the seeds.

6 to 8 servings

INGREDIENTS

- 2 pounds venison sirloin, top round or "better" cuts, trimmed of fat and sinew
- salt and pepper
- 3 ears fresh sweet corn, shucked
- 3 red bell peppers, quartered and seeded
- 1 large sweet yellow onion, sliced into thick slices
- ¼ cup olive oil

- 2 tablespoons red wine vinegar
- 4 large tomatoes, halved and seeded
- 1½ quarts chicken broth
- 2 garlic cloves, minced
- ½ teaspoon dried oregano leaves
- 2 tablespoons fresh parsley leaves, minced
- ¼ teaspoon salt
- ¼ teaspoon black pepper

1. Place venison between plastic wrap or in a zipper-lock bag, and pound lightly until very thin. Season with salt and pepper, and place in a large bowl. Place corn, peppers and onion in the bowl. Drizzle olive oil and vinegar oil, and toss to coat all. While tossing, season with additional salt and pepper.

2. Place venison, corn, peppers, onion and tomatoes on a white-hot grill, and grill on all sides of each. Remove venison when just-cooked, and allow to cool before slicing into 1-inch thick strips.

3. Remove corn kernels from cob, dice peppers, tomatoes and onion, and place in a stock pot. Add chicken broth, garlic and oregano. Bring to a boil over medium-high heat, reduce heat to low, and simmer for 10 minutes. Add venison and parsley, and heat for 1 minute. Season to taste with salt and pepper.

Neck Roast and Beer Stew

There's a ton of flavor in an often-discarded venison neck roast. Browned and simmered until it falls off the bone, it's some of the best tasting meat that ever came out of a deer. Needless to say, the neck of a young animal will take considerably less time to cook than that of a big buck. The neck roast will get really tough before it finally gives in and starts getting tender. You can't rush it. It's best to plan well ahead and get the neck-simmering part out of the way a day, a week or several months earlier. When the meat is pulled from the neck, it can be frozen for later use. For a deeper, more pronounced beer flavor, use a darker beer.

6 to 8 servings, depending on the size of the neck roast

INGREDIENTS

- 1 3- to 5-pound-venison neck roast
- olive oil
- salt and pepper
- 2 to 3 cans beer
- 1½ cups uncooked bacon, diced
- 2 cups green onion, chopped
- 2 cups carrots, diced
- 2 cloves garlic, minced
- 1 tablespoon fresh rosemary leaves, minced
- 2 tablespoons butter
- 3 tablespoons flour

- 12 ounces beer
- 1 quart beef or venison stock
- 1 pound mushrooms, any variety, sliced
- 2 tablespoons tomato paste
- 2 tablespoons grainy mustard
- 1½ tablespoons Worcestershire sauce
- 1 teaspoon salt
- ½ teaspoon pepper
- warm, crusty bread

1. Prepare neck roast in advance. Preheat oven to 375 degrees. Rub roast liberally with olive oil, salt and pepper. Place in a lightly greased roasting pan, and roast in the preheated oven for 1½ to 2 hours, turning occasionally to brown all sides. Add beer to pan, scraping bottom to dislodge bits. Reduce heat to 325, cover with lid or foil. Check after 3 hours to make sure that there is still at least ½ inch of liquid in the bottom of the pan. If not, add more beer. The liquid is essential to breaking down the meat within the roast. Keep checking every hour or so to make sure that there is enough liquid in the pan and to monitor doneness of the meat. When meat pulls away from the bone very easily, usually after 7 to 8 hours in the oven, remove from the oven, and cool to the touch. When cooled, strip meat from the roast and reserve.

2. Cook bacon about halfway in a large pot over medium heat. Add onion, carrot, garlic and rosemary. Cook for 5 minutes, stirring occasionally. Add butter and heat until melted. Sprinkle flour over, stir to coat vegetables with flour, and cook for 4 to 5 minutes more, stirring occasionally, to cook the flour taste out. The flour will help to thicken the finished stew.

3. Add stock, bring to a boil, then reduce heat to medium-low. Add mushrooms, tomato paste, Worcestershire sauce, salt, pepper and reserved cooked neck meat. Simmer until mushrooms are tender.

4. Serve in bowls with warm bread on the side.

Vidalia Onion Soup and Blue Cheese Toast

The state vegetable of Georgia, the Vidalia onion is sweet, not hot. I've taken bites out of raw ones. Try that with a standard yellow onion. Available April through late fall, get 'em while you can. If they're unavailable, substitute another variety of sweet onion. In a pinch, standard onions can be sweetened while sautéing with brown sugar or honey. Cubed venison simmers in the oniony, beefy broth before topping with a crusty blue cheese toast. Talk about flavor!

10 to 12 servings

INGREDIENTS

- 2 tablespoons olive oil
- 3 cups venison, cut into 1-inch cubes
- salt and pepper
- 3 tablespoons butter
- 5 pounds Vidalia onions, thinly sliced
- 2 teaspoons dry thyme
- 6 cloves garlic, finely chopped
- ¼ teaspoon crushed red pepper flakes
- 2 quarts beef broth
- ½ cup dry sherry
- 2 tablespoons Worcestershire sauce

BLUE CHEESE TOAST

- 1 sourdough baguette
- olive oil
- 1 cup blue cheese, crumbled

1. Prepare blue cheese toast. Slice baguette into 1-inch-thick slices, and arrange on baking sheet. Brush a light coating of olive oil over exposed side of the slices. Sprinkle blue cheese over top, and lightly brown in a 325-degree oven.

2. Heat olive oil in a large stock pot or Dutch oven. Season venison with salt and pepper, add to the pot and brown evenly. Add butter, onions, thyme, garlic and red pepper flakes. Reduce heat to low, and simmer for 10 minutes. Add broth, sherry and Worcestershire sauce. Cover and simmer for 1 hour or until venison is tender.

3. To serve, ladle soup into bowls, and top with blue cheese toast.

Portuguese Stew

When the tasty Portuguese sausage is browned and the fat is rendered into the pot, the venison is seared in the same juicy fat, absorbing all the sausage goodness. Take your time, and make sure the sausage and the venison are evenly browned. The rest of the cooking part is easy. If you can't find linguica or chourico, substitute andouille, Italian or any other uncooked high-flavor sausage.

Any cut of venison will work for this stew, but I wouldn't waste tenderloins or backstraps. Stewing tougher cuts will, with time, result in spoon-tender venison.

6 to 8 servings

INGREDIENTS

- 1 pound uncooked linguica or chourico sausage, diced into ½-inch cubes
- 3 cups venison, cut into 1-inch strips
- 3 tablespoons flour, seasoned with 1 teaspoon salt and ½ teaspoon pepper
- 1 large onion, roughly chopped
- 6 cloves garlic, minced
- 3 celery stalks, roughly chopped
- 1 cup carrot, peeled and diced
- 1½ quarts beef broth
- 2 cups dry red wine
- 2 cups potatoes, diced into 1-inch cubes
- 1 15-ounce can diced tomatoes
- ¼ cup fresh parsley leaves, chopped
- salt and pepper

1. In a large stock pot or Dutch oven over medium heat, brown sausage. Dust meat with seasoned flour, salt and pepper, add to pot, and cook until browned. Add onion, garlic, celery and carrot, and cook for 5 minutes, stirring often.

2. Add beef broth and wine, bring to a boil. Reduce heat, cover and simmer for 30 minutes or until meat is tender. Add potatoes, diced tomatoes and parsley, and simmer for 15 minutes more or until potatoes are soft. Season to taste with salt and pepper.

Backstrap Mushroom Soup

As the name implies, this soup is crammed full of mushrooms. The type of mushrooms you use for this dish is entirely up to your personal preferences, your budget and the availability of the mushrooms. I've also made this soup with rehydrated wild mushrooms, and it's just as delicious. The backstrap is grilled, but it can also be pan-seared or broiled, as long as it's not overcooked before adding to the soup. I usually use lesser cuts of venison for soups and stews, but I believe the mushrooms deserve an upgrade from stew meat. The soup production starts with bacon, always a great beginning, and ends with a sprinkling of smoked cheddar cheese.

4 to 6 servings

INGREDIENTS

- 1½ pounds venison backstrap, sliced across grain into ½-inch thick rounds
- olive oil
- 1 teaspoon garlic powder
- salt and pepper
- 2 slices bacon, diced
- 1 cup red onion, diced
- 1 cup carrots, finely diced
- 1 cup parsnip, peeled and finely diced
- 2 garlic cloves, minced
- 2 sprigs fresh rosemary
- 1 quart beef or venison stock
- 2 tablespoons soy sauce
- 2 tablespoons tomato paste
- 4 cups mushrooms, stems trimmed at base and halved
- ½ cup shredded smoked cheddar cheese

1. Prepare backstrap. Rub meat with olive oil, and season with garlic powder, salt and pepper. Place on a white-hot grill, and sear on both sides, but not past medium-rare, about 2 minutes per side. Remove from heat, and let rest at room temperature. When cooled, cut into 1-inch chunks.

2. In a large pot over medium heat, lightly brown bacon. Add onion, carrot, parsnip and garlic. Cook for 4 to 5 minutes. Add rosemary, stock, soy sauce and tomato paste. Bring to a boil, reduce heat to low and simmer for 15 minutes. Add mushrooms, and simmer until soft, but not limp and overcooked. Add venison, and cook for 2 minutes.

3. Remove rosemary sprigs, ladle soup into bowls and top with shredded cheese.

Venistrone Soup

This hearty soup has always been a personal favorite. Cuts from the shoulder, neck and shanks are best suited to slow-cooking with liquid to break down otherwise tough cuts of meat, perfect for my own simplified version of the classic Italian minestrone soup.

8 to 10 servings

INGREDIENTS

- 2½ to 3 pounds venison stew meat, trimmed and cut into 1-inch cubes
- salt and pepper
- 3 tablespoons vegetable oil
- 1 yellow onion, coarsely chopped
- 6 garlic cloves, minced
- 2 quarts beef broth
- ½ cup dry red wine
- 2 cups diced tomatoes, fresh or canned
- 2 bay leaves
- ½ teaspoon each oregano leaves and dried basil
- 1½ cups carrots, diced
- 1 cup celery, diced
- 1½ cups canned kidney beans
- 1 cup canned garbanzo beans
- 1 cup uncooked elbow macaroni
- Parmesan cheese, freshly grated

1. Season venison with salt and pepper. Heat oil over medium heat in a large stock pot, and add venison, cooking until evenly browned. Add onion and garlic, and cook for a few minutes more. Add next 7 ingredients, bring to a boil, then reduce heat to low. Cover and simmer until meat begins to break apart easily, about 1½ to 2 hours. Add pasta and cook, uncovered, until al dente, about 12 minutes. Season to taste with salt and pepper. Serve in bowls and top with Parmesan cheese.

Spicy Sausage, Wild Rice and Kale Stew

This recipe includes spicy venison sausage, but any venison sausage, spicy or not, will do. If your venison sausage is a milder variety, throw in a pinch or two of red pepper flakes to spice it up. Wild rice is a watergrass seed. It's nutty, chewy and often paired with "regular" rice to give it body and softness. Feel free to substitute any wild rice blend, but prepare 1 cup of uncooked rice blend as per the directions on the package.

If kale is not on your list of favorite dark, leafy greens, replace it with spinach or any other greens that make the list.

6 to 8 servings

INGREDIENTS

- 1½ cups water
- 1 teaspoon salt
- ½ cup wild rice
- 1 tablespoon olive oil
- 1 pound spicy venison sausage, broken up or diced
- 1 cup onion, chopped
- 3 cloves garlic, minced
- 1 teaspoon dried oregano
- 1 teaspoon dried basil
- 1½ quarts chicken, beef or venison stock
- 3 cups kale, chopped
- 2 cups seeded and diced fresh tomato
- salt and pepper
- sour cream

1. Prepare wild rice. Bring water to a boil in a medium saucepan over medium-high heat. Add wild rice and salt, cover, reduce heat to low and simmer for 1 hour.

2. Heat oil in a large pot over medium heat. Add sausage and cook until browned, breaking up any large pieces. Add onion, garlic, oregano, basil and chicken stock. Bring to a boil, add kale, reduce heat and simmer until kale is soft, about 5 minutes.

3. Add cooked wild rice and tomato. Simmer for 4 to 5 minutes. Season with salt and pepper and top with a dollop of sour cream.

Four Bean Soup

Oh sure, "three bean" — you hear that all the time. This soup is one bean better, but instead of green, waxed and kidney beans, it's loaded with white beans, lima beans, garbanzo beans and black beans. Of course, if you have alternate favorite bean choices, go nuts. It's your soup. Regarding the beans, you have choices — canned, fresh or dried? My first choice is always fresh and then dried. I'll adjust the type of beans used in the recipe depending on the type of fresh beans I can get my hands on.

This soup has bacon, which adds smoky flavor and fat. If you want to take the flavor thing a few steps further, toss a smoked pork bone into the pot to simmer.

8 servings

INGREDIENTS

- ¼ cup each dried garbanzo (chickpeas), white beans, lima beans and black beans (or any 4 varieties of dried beans)
- 2 teaspoons kosher salt (or 1½ teaspoons table salt)
- ½ pound smoked bacon, diced
- 3 cups venison stew meat, cut into 1-inch cubes
- 2 cups yellow onion, diced
- 1 cup carrots, diced
- 1 cup celery, diced
- 3 garlic cloves, minced
- 1 teaspoon black pepper
- 1 28-ounce can diced tomatoes
- 2 quarts chicken stock
- 4 cups cabbage, chopped
- ¼ cup fresh basil leaves, chopped
- ¼ cup fresh Italian parsley leaves, chopped
- 2 tablespoons freshly squeezed lemon juice
- dash or two Tabasco

1. Soak the beans. Place beans in a large bowl, cover with cold water, and soak for 10 to 12 hours in the refrigerator. Drain and place in a large pot with 2 quarts water and the kosher salt. Bring to a boil, lower heat, and simmer for 1 hour or until beans are tender. Remove from heat, and let beans cool in their liquid.

2. Cook bacon about halfway in a large pot over medium heat. Add venison, and brown evenly in bacon grease. Add onions, carrots, celery, garlic and pepper. Cook for 5 minutes, stirring occasionally. Add chicken stock and tomatoes. Bring to a boil, then lower heat to simmer, cover and cook for 45 minutes.

3. Remove cover, add cabbage, and continue to simmer until meat is tender. Drain beans, and add to pot. Stir in basil, parsley, lemon juice and Tabasco. Season with additional salt to taste.

Italian Meatball Soup

I'm always on the lookout for something to do with a large inventory of ground venison — meatloaf, burger, sausage and, of course, meatballs. The versatility of the meatball is limited only by your imagination. Make it spicy, savory or sweet and sour, but make it with just enough breading to bind it together so that it tastes like a meatball, not a dough ball. If fresh herbs aren't readily available, season the meatballs with Italian seasoning. Although the recipe specifies chicken broth, it works just as well with beef or any game broth or stock. This recipe is a tad long on garlic.

Whenever I prepare meatballs, I always make a large batch and freeze some for later. To keep their shape while frozen, cook and cool the meatballs before placing them in a single layer on a lightly greased baking pan. Place the pan in the freezer, and remove the meatballs when they are completely frozen. For best results, vacuum-package the frozen meatballs while still frozen, and return to the freezer for storage. Simply drop the frozen package into boiling water, and bring to serving temperature.

6 to 8 servings

INGREDIENTS

THE ITALIAN MEATBALL

- 1 pound (about 2 cups), ground venison
- ¼ pound ground pork
- ½ cup onion, minced
- 3 garlic cloves, minced
- ½ cup breadcrumbs
- 1 egg
- ¼ cup milk
- 2 teaspoons fresh oregano, minced
- 1 tablespoon fresh parsley leaves, minced
- ½ teaspoon salt
- ½ teaspoon pepper

THE SOUP

- ¼ cup olive oil
- 1 medium onion, roughly chopped
- 2 celery stalks, diced
- 6 garlic cloves, minced
- 2 carrots, peeled and diced
- ½ teaspoon red pepper flakes
- 1 teaspoon dried basil leaves
- 1 quart plus 3 cups chicken broth
- 1 15-ounce can diced tomatoes
- 4 cups fresh spinach leaves, stems removed
- salt and pepper
- freshly grated Parmesan cheese

1. Prepare meatballs. Preheat oven to 350 degrees. Combine all ingredients in a large bowl, and mix well (preferably with your hands). Divide the mixture into 4 fairly equal portions. Each portion should yield 12 to 15 equal-sized meatballs. Roll them as firmly as possible. Place the meatballs on a lightly greased baking pan, and place in the preheated oven for 5 minutes or until lightly browned. Rotate meatballs to brown evenly, and remove from oven to cool.

2. Heat olive oil in a stock pot over medium heat. Add onion, celery, garlic, carrot, red pepper flakes and basil leaves, and cook until onions are translucent, about 5 minutes. Add broth and diced tomato, and bring to a boil. Reduce heat to low, and simmer for 5 minutes. Add meatballs to soup, and simmer for 5 minutes more. Add spinach leaves, and simmer for 2 minutes. Season to taste with salt and pepper.

3. To serve, ladle soup into bowls, and top with cheese.

chapter 5

On the Grill

If you want to make friends, slap a hunk of well-seasoned venison onto a white-hot grill, and wait for the wafting aroma to attract a crowd. Neighbors you've never met will look over the fence and ask, "Hey pal (he doesn't know your name), whatcha got cooking?" Close your eyes, and visualize the sound and smell of a piece of grilling venison as the juices hit the coal, with smoke rising into the air. Maybe I'll just cut a little slice off the end and see if it's ready.

To me, a perfect venison steak weighs about 10 ounces, is 1 inch thick and is completely trimmed of silver skin, sinew and anything else that is not muscle. Silver skin and sinew don't break down when cooking and actually impart an unpleasant taste to the finished steak. Remove it before you cook it.

I prefer to marinate venison steaks for grilling, not to mask flavors but to enhance them. There are many marinades on the market that claim to knock out those awful gamey flavors. Properly handled in the field and kitchen, venison shouldn't be off-tasting at all and certainly doesn't require any potent elixir to cover up its natural deliciousness. At the very least, give the meat a good rub with your favorite seasoning, whether it's just salt and pepper or a seasoning blend. Because the meat is lean, I typically combine rubs with olive oil, giving the meat some additional fat.

Yes, what a deer feeds on, whether it's in rut or not, and the specific type of deer will affect how they taste when they come off the grill, but they should all taste great. Even a trophy-sized mule deer shot during the rut and finally found after tracking a 2-mile blood trail can make great table fare — really.

Mixed Grill

You've got a mixed bag of venison parts, but not quite enough of any one cut of meat to serve your guests. Restaurants do it all the time: "Tonight, we have a special, our mixed grill." It's also a good sampler dish for your friends who might not have the opportunity to enjoy properly cooked venison. Your inventory will dictate what to throw on the grill. Tougher cuts can benefit from more time in the marinade. Allow six to 12 hours for tougher hindquarter muscles and an hour or two for tenderloins and backstrap medallions. Use your imagination. Got burger? Make a mini-patty for each serving. Venison sausages also make great mixed grill fillers.

INGREDIENTS

- venison steaks, burger, sausage, etc. — amount of each to be determined by freezer inventory
- vegetables for grilling — squash, mushrooms, onions, peppers, etc.

MARINADE
makes 1½ cups, enough to marinate 2 to 3 pounds of meat (4 to 6 servings)

- ⅓ cup onion, chopped
- 3 cloves garlic
- 2 tablespoons fresh rosemary leaves
- ½ cup balsamic vinegar
- 1 tablespoon Worcestershire sauce
- 1 teaspoon kosher salt
- ½ teaspoon black pepper
- ¾ cup olive oil

1. In a food processor or blender, process all marinade ingredients except olive oil, and pulse until smooth. While motor is running, add olive oil in a thin stream until emulsified.

2. Slice thicker vegetables like squash and onions into ¼-inch thick slices. Seed and quarter peppers, and trim the bottoms from mushrooms. Place in a large bowl with venison. Pour marinade over, toss to coat, and refrigerate for 2 to 12 hours, depending on the cut of venison.

3. Remove venison and vegetables from marinade, and drain well. Allow to rest at room temperature for 30 minutes before grilling. Place venison and vegetables on a medium-hot grill until just cooked, but not overcooked. Serve on individual plates or on a large platter "family style."

Blue Cheese Burger

Compared to beef, ground venison can be a bit bland. Because it is so very lean, with about ⅓ of the fat content of ground beef, it can be dry and chewy when cooked. Overcooked ground meat can be muttony and stronger tasting than burger that has been cooked medium-rare. I always add some ground fatty meat to my ground venison to add flavor and moisture. In this instance, I have used a creamy cheese, onions and mushrooms.

4 big burgers

INGREDIENTS

- 1½ pounds ground venison
- 2 tablespoons butter
- 2 cloves garlic, minced
- 1 medium onion, finely diced
- 2 cups mushrooms, coarsely chopped
- ½ cup blue cheese crumbles
- 2 tablespoons breadcrumbs
- salt and pepper
- 4 burger buns
- 4 lettuce leaves
- 4 slices tomato

1. Melt butter in a medium skillet over medium heat. Add onion and garlic until onions are translucent. Stir in mushrooms, and sauté until soft. Transfer to a medium bowl, and allow to cool. Add ground venison, blue cheese, breadcrumbs, salt and pepper, and mix well with your hands to blend.

2. Form into 4 large patties. Grill, pan-fry or broil patties until browned. Add to bun with lettuce, tomato and your choice of other condiments.

Open-Faced Roasted Pepper Swiss Burger

Flame-roasted peppers will spice up your venison burger while adding needed moisture without added fat. Choose your peppers depending on how spicy you like your burgers. In a pinch, roasted peppers available in jars from your grocer will work, but make sure you drain them well before processing, or they will be too wet and won't hold together when cooked. I've been known to char my peppers over the gas stovetop in my home kitchen. Hold the peppers with tongs directly over the flame until blackened. OK, so you have to be careful not to catch the peppers on fire or mess up the range with burnt bits of peppers.

To keep the burger together when cooked, wrap the raw venison in paper towels for 10 minutes, and press together to wick out as much blood as possible.

4 servings

INGREDIENTS

- 1 bell pepper, any color
- 1 jalapeño pepper
- 1 pound ground venison
- ¼ cup Italian breadcrumbs
- ½ teaspoon kosher salt
- ½ teaspoon ground pepper
- 4 slices Swiss cheese
- 3 tablespoons olive oil
- 2 garlic cloves, minced
- 4 thick slices sourdough bread
- ¼ cup mayonnaise
- 1 tablespoon freshly squeezed lemon juice
- 1 tablespoon fresh basil leaves, minced
- red leaf lettuce
- 4 thick slices tomato

1. Place peppers over an open flame grill or burner, and blacken on all sides. Place in a paper bag, and roll up opening to steam peppers, and loosen charred skin. After 10 minutes, remove peppers from bag, scrape burnt skin away with a paper towel or the backside of a knife. Seed peppers and mince.

2. Add minced peppers to a large bowl. Add venison, breadcrumbs, salt and pepper. Mix thoroughly with your hands. Form into 4 equal balls. OK, now this might sound a little goofy. Toss the burger balls back and forth into your hands like you would a baseball into a mitt. It will compress the meat and make it hold together better while cooking. Press each ball lightly into a patty, about 1 inch thick.

3. Combine olive oil and garlic, and brush over one side of the sourdough bread slices.

4. Grill or broil sourdough bread until lightly browned on the oiled side. Grill or pan-sear burgers over medium heat until cooked to desired doneness. Place cheese on top and cook until melted.

5. Combine mayonnaise, lemon juice and basil. Place bread on plates, toasted side up. Top with lettuce, tomato, burger and a dollop of mayonnaise mixture.

Grilled Venison with Sweet Mustard Sauce

This recipe will work with steaks cut from the hindquarter muscles of young animals and, of course, tenderloins and backstraps. The sweet mustard sauce is great on just about any hunk of meat.

4 servings

INGREDIENTS

- 4 8- to 10-ounce venison steaks, trimmed of all silver skin, fat and gristle
- 2 tablespoons olive oil
- ¼ cup dry red wine
- 2 cloves garlic, minced
- 2 tablespoons fresh herbs — rosemary, oregano, basil, sage, etc.
- 2 tablespoons green peppercorns, crushed
- 2 tablespoons olive oil
- ½ teaspoon kosher salt

SWEET MUSTARD SAUCE

- ½ cup Dijon mustard
- ½ cup red currant jelly
- 1 lemon, juice only
- 1 tablespoon chopped sage

1. In a small bowl, combine all sweet mustard sauce ingredients, and mix well.

2. In another small bowl, combine olive oil with next 6 ingredients to make marinade. Place steaks in a baking dish, and pour marinade over. Cover and refrigerate for 2 to 3 hours.

3. Remove meat from refrigerator, and let sit at room temperature for 30 minutes. Heat a large skillet over medium-high heat. Add steaks, and brown on all sides, but not past medium-rare. Allow to rest for 5 minutes and top with sweet mustard sauce.

Horseradish Sauce

If it's good enough for prime rib, it's sure to be good on a piece of grilled deer meat. This is the long version of one of my favorite sauces. Serve on the side or across the top of grilled venison.

makes about ⅓ cup, enough for 4 grilled steaks

INGREDIENTS

- 1 tablespoon olive oil
- 2 green onions, diced
- 1 garlic clove, minced
- 1 teaspoon fresh rosemary leaves, minced (or substitute pinch dried rosemary leaves)
- ¼ cup dry white wine
- ½ teaspoon Worcestershire sauce
- 2 to 3 tablespoons prepared horseradish
- ¾ cup heavy (whipping) cream

1. Heat olive oil in a small saucepan over medium heat. Add green onions, garlic and rosemary, and cook for 1 minute. Add white wine and Worcestershire sauce, and reduce liquid by ½. Stir in horseradish and cream, and bring to a boil. Reduce heat to low, and simmer until liquid is reduced to about ⅓ cup.

Go-To Grilling Marinade

With just a hint of Asian flavors, this is a good everyday marinade with sweet and sour components. Marinate venison steaks 1 to 6 hours.

About 2 cups

INGREDIENTS

- ¾ cup oil
- ½ cup honey
- ¼ cup red wine vinegar
- ⅓ cup soy sauce
- 1 tablespoon garlic powder
- 1½ teaspoons ground ginger
- 1½ teaspoons salt
- 1 tablespoon coarse ground pepper

1. Combine all ingredients in a tight-fitting jar, and shake. Can be stored in the refrigerator for several weeks.

Raspberry Vinaigrette Marinade and Sauce

If you're short on time and looking for an easy and super-delicious marinade and sauce, this one fits the bill. Soak venison steaks for an hour or so before slapping on a white-hot grill. The sugary raspberry preserves will give the grilled meat crispy caramelized edges. For extra flavor, baste with vinaigrette while grilling, and drizzle a little extra over just before serving.

2 cups vinaigrette

INGREDIENTS

- 2 garlic cloves, minced
- ½ cup raspberry preserves
- ¼ cup balsamic vinegar (or substitute ⅓ cup red wine vinegar)
- ⅓ cup green onions, chopped
- 1 tablespoon Dijon mustard
- 1 cup olive oil

1. In a large bowl, whisk together garlic, preserves, vinegar, onions and mustard. While whisking, add oil in a thin stream until emulsified.

Mockstrap

I often have people mistake my stuffed venison hindquarter cuts for backstraps. If you treat them right, they can be just as tender, especially if they're removed from a young doe. The first step is to separate each muscle from the hindquarter. Using a sharp boning knife, work along the sinew that separates the muscle groups, and remove each muscle as intact as possible. Clean it up by trimming away anything that isn't muscle. If it's whitish in color, it's got to go. Trim sirloin and round steaks parallel to the grain into 3- to 4-inch-wide strips, about the same width and thickness as a backstrap. It might take a few pieces of the various muscles to make 4 serving-sized portions. If you are not too adept at tying up a stuffed piece of meat with butcher string, you can also secure with skewers or toothpicks.

Don't waste the trimmed sinewy parts. Throw them into a lightly oiled pan until brown. Stir in some celery, carrot, onion and herbs, and cook for a few minutes more. Deglaze the pan with a big glug of red wine, perhaps some balsamic vinegar, and let it simmer for an hour or so, adding more wine as needed. Strain the solids through a colander and return the liquid to the pan. Whisk in some chilled butter, and spoon over cooked venison.

4 servings

INGREDIENTS

- 2 pounds round steak, eye of round or sirloin (read preparation info on Page 96)
- olive oil
- salt and pepper
- 4 deli-thin slices of prosciutto
- 2 cups raw spinach leaves, stems removed
- 1 cup Monterey Jack cheese, shredded
- 3 tablespoons breadcrumbs
- butcher string

1. To butterfly venison, lay out on a flat cutting surface. The idea is to open the meat up, leaving a "hinge" in the center. Start with a sharp, thin-bladed knife, and cut into the meat just below one end. Continue to cut into the meat while sliding the knife toward the opposite end of the meat, but not all the way through. If you happen to cut too deeply, it's not a huge deal, and you can fix it with a prosciutto "patch." When done, you should be able to open the meat up relatively flat with the hinge in the center of the meat. If the meat is a larger piece, you can butterfly it again and have two hinges. Press the meat flat.

2. Rub venison on both sides with olive oil, and season with salt and pepper. Lay flat with the cut side facing up. Spread prosciutto across venison. Arrange spinach leaves on top of prosciutto. Combine cheese and breadcrumbs, and spread across spinach. Press down on stuffing so it lays flat. Starting at one end, roll up snugly while holding stuffing in place with fingers. Tie securely with butcher string.

3. Place stuffed and tied venison on a medium-hot, well-lubricated grill. Brown on all sides until the internal temperature is 135 degrees for medium-rare. Let rest for 5 minutes, remove string and slice into medallions. If desired, drizzle your favorite sauce over.

Blackberry Chipotle Sauce

Sweet, sour and spicy — a great combination for any dark-fleshed game, like venison. Just how spicy will be determined by how much chipotle pepper you add to the sauce.

You can buy chipotle peppers in a can. They're hot, but not quite as hot as the adobo sauce they're packed in. You can also purchase dried chipotle peppers and reconstitute them in hot water for about 30 minutes. Drain and chop. In a pinch, a splash or two of chipotle-flavored Tabasco will work. Spoon over grilled venison, or serve on the side as a dipping sauce.

INGREDIENTS

- 1 tablespoon olive oil
- ¼ cup yellow onion, minced
- 2 garlic cloves, minced
- ¼ cup balsamic vinegar
- 1 cup dry red wine
- 1 tablespoon blackberry preserves
- 1 tablespoon chipotle pepper (see above), minced
- 1 teaspoon cornstarch mixed with equal part cold water
- salt and pepper

1. Heat olive oil in a medium saucepan over medium heat. Add onion and garlic, and sauté for 3 to 4 minutes. Add vinegar, wine, blackberry preserves and chipotle pepper. Bring to a boil, reduce heat to low and simmer for 5 minutes. Stir in cornstarch mixture, and bring to a boil to thicken. Remove from heat, and season to taste with salt and pepper.

2. Sauce can be served as is or processed until smooth in a blender.

Three Simple Grilling Sauces

You've got to love it when you stumble upon a recipe that only needs a handful of ingredients, is simple to prepare and, best, tastes great. Chances are good that you won't bother with a three-page recipe with a long list of obscure ingredients that you can't even pronounce. Here are some easy sauces that'll get you in and out of the kitchen at warp speed.

SPICY RED CURRANT AND MUSTARD SAUCE

Baste on grilled venison a few minutes before done, and serve with additional sauce on the side.

about 1 cup

INGREDIENTS

- ⅔ cup red currant jelly
- ⅓ cup Dijon mustard
- 1 teaspoon lemon juice
- 1 teaspoon red pepper flakes

1. Combine all ingredients, and mix well.

ORANGE-GINGER SAUCE

A little sweet, a little sour and just salty enough.

about 1¼ cups sauce

INGREDIENTS

- ⅔ cup orange juice concentrate
- ⅓ cup soy sauce
- ¼ cup rice vinegar
- 2 tablespoons pickled ginger, minced

1. Whisk together, and drizzle over cooked venison.

APRICOT-HORSERADISH SAUCE

Several years ago, someone described this sauce to me, and it sounded a little goofy, but that's not necessarily a bad thing. I made a few mental notes, which are often unreliable, and came up with this sauce.

about 1 cup

INGREDIENTS

- ½ cup prepared horseradish
- ½ cup apricot preserves
- 1 tablespoon lemon juice

1. Combine ingredients, and spoon over grilled venison a few minutes before removing from heat.

Two Great Salsas

A departure from traditional tomato salsas, these are two of my favorite grilled venison toppers. After preparing the salsas, let them stand at room temperature for an hour to blend flavors and give them a chance to warm up. Putting cold salsa on a hot venison steak just doesn't make good sense.

BLACK BEAN AND MANGO SALSA

about 2 cups

INGREDIENTS

- 1 cup cooked black beans, rinsed and drained
- 1 mango, peeled, seeded and cut into ½-inch cubes
- ¼ cup red onion, finely diced
- 1 jalapeño pepper, seeded and minced
- 2 garlic cloves, minced
- 3 tablespoons fresh basil leaves, minced
- 3 tablespoons freshly squeezed lime juice
- 2 tablespoons granulated sugar
- 2 tablespoons olive oil
- salt and pepper

1. Combine all ingredients, and season to taste with salt and pepper.

CHERRY TOMATO AND GREEN OLIVE SALSA

Homegrown tomatoes are one of my favorite foods, but unless you grow them or have a good friend who does, you have to rely on grocery stores. Farmers' markets and roadside stands can be good sources when in season. In January, be very suspicious of a "vine-ripened" tomato. During cold-weather months, I rely on cherry tomatoes to get my fix. It's hit or miss, but they can be much sweeter than the larger varieties.

about 1½ cups

INGREDIENTS

- 1 cup cherry tomatoes, halved
- ¼ cup pitted green olives, sliced
- 2 green onions, minced
- 1 tablespoon fresh oregano leaves, minced
- 2 tablespoons fresh cilantro leaves, minced
- 1 tablespoon freshly squeezed lemon juice
- 1 tablespoon balsamic vinegar
- 1 teaspoon chili powder
- 1 teaspoon honey
- salt and pepper

1. Combine all ingredients, and season to taste with salt and pepper.

One Great Venison Steak

It doesn't happen that often anymore, but I have had well-meaning folks bring me bone-in, gristly deer steaks that are about a foot in diameter. Some misguided soul has taken a deer hindquarter or, even worse, shoulder roast and cut it into steaks with a band saw. If all you plan to do is cut it up and throw it in the slow cooker, I suppose it'll do, but there really is a much better way to create a mouth-watering, tender venison steak.

This steak is topped with a compound butter, which is just a softened butter with some crumbled blue cheese, chives and garlic mixed in. I keep an assortment of compound butters in my freezer for grilled fish and game. Picture a hot, seared venison steak topped with a melting disc of flavorful butter running down the sides. Not only does it look and taste great, it contributes added fat to an otherwise very lean piece of meat.

4 servings

- 4 10-ounce venison steaks
- 2 tablespoons olive oil
- ½ cup dry red wine
- 2 garlic cloves, minced
- 1 tablespoon fresh rosemary leaves, minced
- ½ teaspoon Kosher salt
- ½ teaspoon black pepper

BLUE CHEESE COMPOUND BUTTER

- ½ pound softened salted butter
- ⅔ cup crumbled blue cheese
- ¼ cup fresh chives, minced (or sub green onions)
- 2 garlic cloves, minced
- waxed paper, foil or plastic wrap

1. Prepare blue cheese compound butter. Combine all ingredients in a bowl, and blend with a spatula. Transfer to the center of a 12-inch sheet of waxed paper, foil or plastic wrap, and form into a rectangle about 4 to 5 inches long and 2 inches wide. Roll waxed paper over butter, forming a cylinder. Twist paper at both ends and place in the freezer for 1 hour or until very firm.

2. Combine olive oil, wine, garlic, rosemary, salt and pepper in a bowl or zipper lock bag. Add steaks, and refrigerate for 3 to 4 hours. Remove steaks from marinade, and let rest at room temperature for 20 minutes before grilling. Re-season with additional salt and pepper. Remove compound butter from freezer.

3. Place steaks on a white-hot, well-lubricated grill for about 3 minutes per side for medium-rare. Transfer to a platter, cover loosely with a foil tent, and let the steaks rest for 5 minutes. While steaks are resting, slice butter into 4¼-inch thick rounds. To serve, place steaks on plates, and top with compound butter.

chapter 6

In the Oven

I was raised on casseroles. OK, maybe not every night, but I'm willing to bet that we ate something baked or roasted four or five nights a week. From broccoli casserole to something called "hamburger pie," dinner was usually served from a baking dish. My mother couldn't have been happier than the day she discovered Hamburger Helper.

The Food Network changed everything. Cooks are now called chefs, elevating their social status but not necessarily their standard of living. The explosion of TV cooking shows has encouraged home cooks to shop, chop and roll their ingredients into something fitting for a food magazine cover. Although I'm sure sales of canned creamed soups haven't fallen off much since Mom used to make dinner, the "foodies" are moving past canned-food-inspired casseroles to dishes using fresher and more colorful ingredients. We all hear how important it is for food to look good. "We eat with our eyes first." Obviously, it might look like a magazine cover, but it still has to taste good.

When it comes to cooking venison, I probably use my oven least of all. Given the choice between a roasted backstrap and one cooked on a smoky hot grill, I'll opt for the latter. Virtually anything that can be cooked in an oven can be prepared in an outdoor cooker with a lid. Controlling the temperature of a grill isn't quite as exact as an indoor oven, but it's usually close enough. Ovens are best used when you need to make tougher cuts tender. Necks, shoulders, hindquarter roasts, ribs and shanks can all benefit from slow-roasting in a shallow bath of something flavorful. Eventually, they will all succumb to moist heat and go from hockey puck to spoon-tender. If your venison roast is tough and chewy, keep cooking. It'll get there.

No Problemo Shoulder Roast

I'd like to get back the hours spent excising usable pieces of stew meat from deer shoulders. It's work best left to those who do it for a living. I'd rather spend my time doing something, anything, else. Fortunately, there's a way to remove the meat from a bone-in deer shoulder that requires minimal knife skills. I let my oven do most of the work.

This version of my basic slow-cooked shoulder roast recipe has a little sweet and a little heat, but not so much of either that it should bother anyone. The basic premise is that anything cooked long enough at low temperature with some liquid will eventually get tender. Besides convenience, that's one of the reasons that slow-cookers like the Crock Pot have become so popular among those of us who shoot animals. Even tougher cuts of venison that sit in a hot pot of some kind of liquid all day will eventually get tender. The problem with a big deer shoulder is that they don't make slow-cookers big enough to fit them, at least not for the home cook. As long as you have an oven or even an outdoor cooker with a lid, you're golden.

INGREDIENTS

- 1 venison shoulder
- olive oil
- beer, wine, or any type of stock
- 2 onions, quartered
- 3 carrots, chopped into large pieces
- 3 celery ribs, chopped into large pieces

THE RUB

Make a big batch of rub that you can use now and later.

- 1 cup kosher or sea salt
- ¼ cup dark brown sugar
- 3 tablespoons paprika
- ¼ cup garlic powder
- ¼ cup onion powder
- 3 tablespoons pepper
- 1 tablespoon dry mustard

1. Prepare rub mixture.

2. Pat shoulder dry with cloth or paper towels. Rub it liberally with olive oil, then rub. Wrap it with plastic wrap, and refrigerate 12 to 24 hours. Place it in a lightly greased heavy-duty baking pan. Add onion, carrots and celery to the pan.

3. Place the uncovered baking pan in a preheated 375-degree oven, and roast until evenly browned on both sides, about 30 minutes per side. Add about 1 inch of liquid (beer, wine, stock) to the pan. Cover tightly with a lid or heavy duty foil, and lower the temperature to 325 degrees. Depending on the size of the shoulder, the next step can take up to 6 to 8 hours.

4. After a couple of hours, check the pan, and add liquid if needed. Check again in another 2 hours then every hour after until the meat starts to pull away from the bone easily. It's not done until the bone can be easily removed. When it is done, the bone will pull cleanly away from the meat.

5. Allow meat to cool, and enjoy now as you would any pot roast, or collect and cool chunks of meat for refrigerator or freezer storage. Meat can also be used for tacos, enchiladas, quick soups or laced with a spirited barbecue sauce and piled high in a bun for a great sandwich.

Bacon-Wrapped Backstrap

It's not what you think. This recipe takes the relationship between bacon and venison to a whole new level. Picture a seasoned venison backstrap, topped with chopped mushrooms and totally encased in crispy bacon. If your deer was a small one, you might have to use a pair of backstraps. Since the recipe specifies the center cut of the meat, save the trimmed ends for a tasty appetizer to snack on while you're waiting for the main course. Lemon zest is the yellow skin of the fruit, shaved and minced. To remove it, skin closely with a vegetable peeler or zester. A meat thermometer plays an important role with this dish. If you don't own one, you should.

4 servings

INGREDIENTS

- 2 tablespoons butter
- 3 cups mushrooms, chopped
- 2 garlic cloves, minced
- ¼ cup fresh Italian parsley, minced
- 1 teaspoon lemon zest
- 3 tablespoons breadcrumbs, any variety
- 1 pound venison backstrap, cut from the center section
- salt and pepper
- 1 pound thin-sliced bacon

1. Preheat oven to 375 degrees. Melt butter in a saucepan over medium heat. Add mushrooms and garlic, and sauté until mushrooms are soft. Stir in parsley, lemon zest and breadcrumbs. Allow to cool completely.

2. Season venison with salt and pepper. On a flat surface, lay half of the bacon strips out, leaving a bacon-width gap between each slice. Weave the other half of the bacon strips in an over-and-under or checkerboard pattern to create a woven bacon pattern. Place the backstrap on the center of the bacon. Spread the mushroom mixture on top of the backstrap. Bring the sides of the bacon up to the top and overlap to seal.

3. Place the bacon-encased backstrap, seam side down, on a baking sheet. Place in the preheated oven for 10 minutes or until bacon is evenly browned. Check internal temperature with a meat thermometer. It should be about 120 degrees. Flip over to brown seam side, and continue to cook until internal temperature is 135 degrees for medium-rare, 150 for medium and 165 or more for overcooked.

4. Remove meat from oven, let rest for a few minutes to firm up bacon. Slice into 4 servings.

Apple-Stuffed Backstrap

Backstraps can be stuffed with just about anything you can imagine — asparagus, roasted bell pepper, your favorite cheese, mushrooms, ham, cream cheese, dried fruit and anything else that honks your horns. This is one of my favorite combinations that's sweet, sour, cheesy and spicy.

Serves 2 to 4 (depending on the size of the backstrap)

INGREDIENTS

- 1 venison backstrap, trimmed of all silver skin
- olive oil
- 1 medium apple, diced
- ¼ cup red onion, diced
- 2 garlic cloves, minced
- 1 teaspoon lemon juice
- 1 small jalapeño pepper, seeded and minced
- 1 tablespoon brown sugar
- ¼ cup shredded Parmesan cheese
- butcher string

1. Lay the backstrap on a flat cutting surface. The idea is to open the meat up, leaving a "hinge" in the center. It's called "butterflying" the meat. Start with a sharp, thin-bladed knife, and cut into the meat just below the smaller end. You want to leave the small end uncut so it will hold the stuffing in when tied. Continue to cut into the meat while sliding the knife toward the opposite end of the backstrap, but not all the way through. If you happen to cut too deeply, it's not a huge deal, and you can fix it. When done, you should be able to open the backstrap up relatively flat with the hinge in the center of the meat. If your backstrap is a larger piece, you can butterfly it again.

2. Heat a thin layer of oil in a skillet over medium-hot heat. Add apple, onion, garlic, lemon juice and jalapeño pepper. Sauté for 2 to 3 minutes. Sprinkle brown sugar over. You may also add a little more lemon juice over if you like your stuffing more tart. Allow mixture to cool. Mix with cheese.

3. Rub some olive oil into the meat, and season with salt and pepper. Lay seasoned backstrap flat, with the inside facing up. Spread stuffing over meat, and press down to flatten. Leave the outside edges "unstuffed" so that, when tied, the meat will bind together. Roll the meat up on one end, and secure with butcher string. While pressing stuffing into meat, continue to hold together snugly while securing with string.

4. Heat a thin layer of oil in a medium-hot skillet. Brown meat on all sides, and remove when medium-rare. While skillet is still over heat, add a splash or two of white or red wine, and stir to deglaze pan. Remove from heat and whisk in 4 to 5 tablespoons of chilled butter (we're making sauce). Allow to rest for a few minutes before removing string. Using a sharp, thin-bladed knife, slice meat into medallions. Arrange on plates, and drizzle sauce over.

Fig-Glazed Roast

I usually keep a jar of balsamic vinegar-infused figs on hand. The mildly sweet figs pair well with the not-so-acidic vinegar. Add a sprig or two of fresh sage or rosemary and a few garlic cloves, and it's an instant pan sauce. This balsamic-fig combo is one you'll want to use again and again on any dark-fleshed game.

6 to 8 servings

INGREDIENTS

- 1 3- to 4-pound venison roast, bone-in or out
- ½ teaspoon salt
- ½ teaspoon pepper
- 1 teaspoon dried sage
- ¾ cup dry red wine
- ⅔ cup dried figs, thinly sliced into matchsticks
- ¼ pound (1 stick) chilled unsalted butter, cut into small pieces

FIG GLAZE

- 1 13-ounce jar fig preserves
- 2 tablespoons lemon juice
- 1 tablespoon Dijon mustard
- ½ cup balsamic vinegar
- ½ teaspoon salt
- ¼ teaspoon pepper

1. Prepare glaze. Heat all ingredients in a saucepan over low heat to blend flavors. Save saucepan for Step 3.

2. Preheat oven to 325 degrees. Season roast liberally with salt, pepper and sage. Place in a lightly greased roasting pan in the preheated oven for 1 hour. Remove roast from oven, baste with half of fig glaze. Return to oven, and roast for 45 minutes more. Remove from oven and baste with remaining glaze. Increase oven heat to 400 degrees, and return roast to oven for 15 to 20 minutes or until internal temperature is 135 degrees for medium-rare. Transfer from oven to a cutting board.

3. While roasting pan is still hot, pour red wine into pan, and stir to loosen bits. Transfer contents of pan to the small saucepan used to heat glaze. Heat over low heat, and stir in figs. When hot, remove from heat and whisk in butter pieces until emulsified.

4. Slice roast thinly, arrange on a platter, and spoon sauce over the center of the meat (don't smother the meat with sauce!).

Texas-Style Hindquarter Oven Roast

Blasphemy! Making a "Texas-style" roast indoors just ain't right. Here's the deal. Not everyone owns an outdoor cooker. Others can't get past the snow bank to even find the barbecue, but they'd still like to turn a big deer roast into something that's long on flavor and eats like a pot roast. The process is pretty much the same as cooking it outdoors, and the aroma of the slow-roasted venison will linger in your kitchen long after the meat has been digested. It's best prepared in a heavy-duty roasting pan. A Dutch oven with a lid is ideal.

6 to 8 servings, depending on the size of the roast

INGREDIENTS

- 1 3- to 5-pound venison roast, boneless, tied tightly with butcher string or net
- 1 12-ounce beer
- heavy-duty foil

THE RUB

- ½ cup Kosher salt
- ½ cup coarse ground black pepper
- 2 tablespoons paprika
- 2 tablespoons garlic powder
- 2 tablespoons chili powder

MOP SAUCE

- 2 cups water
- ½ cup lemon juice
- 1 teaspoon kosher salt
- 1 stick butter, melted
- 1 tablespoon granulated garlic
- 1 tablespoon onion powder

1. Prepare rub. Combine rub ingredients in any container, and rub into roast. Wrap the roast snugly with plastic wrap, and place in the refrigerator for 12 to 24 hours.

2. Prepare mop sauce. Combine all ingredients in a bowl. Mop sauce will be applied to roast with a pastry/basting brush or spoon.

3. Preheat oven to 400 degrees. Remove roast from refrigerator, and remove plastic wrap. Place in a roasting pan, and brown evenly on all sides, rotating the roast when browned. When browned, add 1 can beer to the pan. Cover with lid or foil, reduce heat to 325 degrees and cook for 1 hour. Remove lid, and apply mop sauce every 15 to 20 minutes until internal temperature reaches 155 degrees. Remove from oven, and set on a large sheet or two of foil. Baste once more, and wrap with the foil. Place the foil-wrapped roast back in the pan, and return to the oven. Cook for 2 hours more.

Potato Hot Dish

While working on a television show, I wound up in a popular restaurant in Brainerd, Minn., for lunch. One of the featured dishes highlighted on the menu was the "tater tot hot dish," apparently the state casserole. Four out of five of us, the locals, ordered the hot dish. I was the odd man out. Fortunately, I managed to sneak a bite or two from the others. This is weighty, comfortable food that makes you fall asleep on the couch at halftime. In the spirit of the Tater Tot Hot Dish, here's my updated version (on Page 116), made without the aid of canned creamed soup or tater tots.

8 servings

INGREDIENTS

"REAL" CREAM OF MUSHROOM SOUP

- ¼ cup butter
- 1 pound fresh mushrooms, chopped
- 1 cup green onions, chopped
- 2 cloves garlic, minced
- 1 teaspoon fresh rosemary leaves
- 2 tablespoons flour
- 2 cups chicken broth
- 1 cup milk
- 2 tablespoons dry sherry
- salt and pepper to taste

- ½ pound venison or pork Italian sausage, (if using venison sausage, add 1 tablespoon olive oil)
- 1 pound ground venison
- 1 cup onions
- 1 cup carrots, peeled and diced
- 1 cup fresh green beans, cut into 1- to 2-inch lengths
- 1 cup fresh corn kernels
- 2 cups potatoes, peeled and shredded
- salt and pepper
- ½ cup seasoned breadcrumbs
- 1½ cups jack cheese, shredded

1. Melt butter in a saucepan over medium heat. Add mushrooms, green onions, garlic and rosemary. Cook for 2 to 3 minutes. Sprinkle flour over mushroom mixture while stirring. Continue to stir for 3 to 5 minutes more to thicken and cook flour taste out. Add chicken stock, a little at a time while stirring. Stir in milk and sherry. Heat until almost boiling, stirring often. Remove from heat, and season with salt and pepper.

2. Preheat oven to 350 degrees. Brown sausage and venison in a large skillet over medium heat. While cooking, break up sausage, and mix well with venison. Add onions and carrots. Cook for 4 minutes. Stir in green beans and corn, and cook for 1 minute.

3. Transfer contents of skillet into a buttered 9-by-13-inch baking dish. Pour cream of mushroom soup over. In a bowl, season shredded potatoes with salt and pepper, and toss with breadcrumbs and cheese. Spread potato and cheese mixture over top.

4. Place in the preheated oven for 30 to 40 minutes or until cheese and potatoes are lightly browned. Allow to cool and set up for a few minutes before serving.

Southwest Meatloaf

This recipe will add some zip to everyday meatloaf. If you can't find chorizo, a spirited sausage from south of the border, substitute any spicy sausage. If spicy is not your thing, this recipe is probably not for you.

6 to 8 servings

INGREDIENTS

- 2 tablespoons olive oil
- 1 cup onions, finely diced
- 2 jalapeño peppers, seeded and minced
- 6 garlic cloves, minced
- 1½ cups crushed tortilla chips
- 2 eggs, lightly beaten
- 1 cup tomato salsa (your choice of mild, medium or spicy)
- 1½ cups fresh corn kernels
- 1 cup shredded Mexican cheese blend

- 1 teaspoon chili powder
- ½ teaspoon dried oregano
- ¼ teaspoon cumin powder
- 1 teaspoon salt
- 1½ pounds ground venison, elk, etc.
- 1 pound lean ground beef
- ½ pound chorizo sausage, casing removed, crumbled
- 1 cup sour cream
- 3 tablespoons ketchup
- 1 tablespoon lime juice

1. Heat oil in a skillet over medium heat, and add onion, jalapeño pepper and garlic. Sauté until onions are translucent. Allow to cool.

2. In a large bowl, combine tortilla chips with next 8 ingredients, and mix well. Add venison, beef, chorizo and cooled onion mixture. Mix all ingredients thoroughly with your hands.

3. In a lightly oiled loaf pan or baking dish, form into a loaf about 4 inches tall. Bake in a preheated 375-degree oven for 50 to 60 minutes or until internal temperature is 160 degrees. Lightly cover with foil, and allow to rest for 10 minutes before serving.

4. Whisk together sour cream, ketchup and lime juice. To serve, slice meatloaf, and arrange on plates. Top with a dollop of the sour cream mixture.

Herb Crusted Meatloaf

When making meatloaf, I prefer a thicker-ground venison. It gives the cooked meatloaf a firmer texture and holds together better than a smaller grind. Ground veal can be a bit pricey and hard to come by. I've substituted ground beef, turkey or chicken, and it works just fine. The herb crust is also great on roasts.

6 to 8 servings

INGREDIENTS

- 2 cups ground venison
- 2 cups ground veal
- 2 cups ground pork
- 1½ cups onion, finely diced
- 6 garlic cloves, minced
- 2 large eggs
- 1⅓ cups canned diced tomato
- 1 tablespoon chili powder (I prefer ancho or chipotle powder)
- 2 teaspoons kosher salt
- 1 teaspoon coarsely ground black pepper
- 1 cup breadcrumbs (I prefer Japanese panko breadcrumbs)

HERB CRUST

- 1 cup butter, melted
- 1½ cups breadcrumbs
- 2 tablespoons fresh rosemary leaves, minced
- 1 tablespoon fresh thyme, minced
- ½ cup onion, finely diced
- 4 cloves garlic, minced
- ⅓ teaspoon salt
- ¼ teaspoon black pepper

1. Combine meatloaf ingredients in a large bowl, mixing well with your hands. Place into a well-greased baking dish, and form into a rectangle, about 3 inches tall.

2. Combine herb crust ingredients in a bowl, and spread over top of meat mixture. Place dish into a preheated 350-degree oven for 1½ hours or until internal temperature is 160 degrees.

Apple-Braised Neck Roast

Following the usual braising protocol, the venison neck roast is first browned, and then slow-cooked in a shallow liquid bath in a covered container. I've added an additional flavor element by brining the roast for several hours before roasting. This process works just as well with any venison roast. I often hear fellow hunters complain about how neck roasts are tough and stringy. They just didn't cook it long enough. As long as you keep a shallow layer of liquid in the roasting pan and the pan's lid is snug, the meat from your neck roast will eventually be moist and tender. I usually prepare this dish in a Dutch oven, often on the stovetop rather than the oven.

When cooked, strip the meat from the bones, and use for tacos, enchiladas, barbecue sandwiches or just nestled up against a pile of steaming mashed potatoes and smothered in pan sauce.

serving size varies

THE BRINE

- 1 cup kosher salt
- 1 cup brown sugar
- ¼ cup granulated or powdered garlic
- ¼ cup ground black pepper
- 1 cup cider vinegar
- 1 gallon ice water

- 1 venison neck roast
- olive oil
- salt and pepper

THE BRAISE

- 1 quart apple cider
- 2 cups venison or beef stock
- 3 tart apples, quartered
- 1 medium onion, roughly chopped
- 6 garlic cloves, whole
- 2 bay leaves

1. Prepare brine. Heat 2 cups of the water in a saucepan over medium-high heat. Add salt, sugar, granulated garlic and pepper and stir until dissolved. Add to remaining ice water and stir in vinegar. Place roast in a heavy-duty plastic bag, pour brine over and seal bag at opening to immerse roast in brine. Place in a container, and refrigerate for 6 to 12 hours.

2. Remove roast from brine. Discard brine. Rinse roast, pat dry with paper or clean cloth towels. Rub with olive oil, and season with salt and pepper.

3. Preheat oven to 325 degrees. Heat 2 tablespoons olive oil in a large skillet (or Dutch oven) over medium-high heat. Add roast, and brown well on all sides. The browning will enhance flavor!

4. Transfer meat to a well-greased roasting pan (or leave in Dutch oven). Stir cider and stock together, and pour enough in pan to cover ½ to ¾-inch. Add apples, onion, garlic and bay leaves to pan. Cover tightly with heavy foil or lid, and place in the preheated oven.

5. Check oven after 2 hours to make sure there is adequate liquid in the pan. Add as necessary to keep at least ½-inch of liquid at all times. Note: If you got distracted and allowed the liquid to evaporate, just deglaze the pan with additional cider and broth. Depending on the size of the roast, it will take at least 5 hours for the braise. Check every hour or so after the first 2 hours, and continue until meat pulls away from the bone easily.

Shepherd's Cottage Pie

My mother used to make something she called "shepherd's pie" several times a year. It was one of her best dishes, but the best part was watching my dad stir up the potatoes with the tomato sauce, green beans and ground beef. It looked like something a 4-year-old would create, and it drove my mom crazy. I'm pretty sure that's why he did it.

I've since been told that if it's made with beef, it's cottage pie. The same dish made with lamb is shepherd's pie. Because I make mine with ground venison and never really gave it a name, well, it's the best I could come up with. Ground venison is lean, lean, lean. If yours isn't ground with 20 percent fatty beef or pork, add some to the mix. The carrots and onions are grated but could just as easily be diced if you don't want to mess with a grater.

4 to 6 servings

INGREDIENTS

- 1½ pounds red potatoes, skin on or off (I leave it on), quartered
- 3 tablespoons butter
- ¼ sour cream
- 1 egg
- salt and white pepper
- 2 tablespoons olive oil
- 4 cups ground venison
- 1 large carrot, peeled and grated
- 1 large onion, peeled and grated
- 4 cloves garlic, minced
- 2 tablespoons Worcestershire sauce
- 1 tablespoon fresh rosemary leaves, minced
- ½ teaspoon salt
- ½ teaspoon pepper
- 1 cup tomato puree
- ½ cup dry red wine
- 1 cup frozen peas
- ⅓ cup Parmesan cheese
- paprika

1. Boil potatoes in salted water until soft. Drain and mash with butter, sour cream and egg. Season with salt and pepper, and keep warm.

2. Preheat oven to 400 degrees. Heat olive oil in a large skillet over medium heat. Add venison and cook until browned. Stir in carrot, onion and garlic. Cook for 3 minutes. Add Worcestershire sauce, rosemary, salt, pepper, tomato puree and red wine. Cook until liquid is reduced and thickened, about 6 to 8 minutes.

3. Stir in frozen peas, and spoon mixture into a baking dish. Spread potatoes evenly over meat mixture. Sprinkle cheese over top, and lightly sprinkle paprika over cheese. Place in the preheated oven for 15 minutes or until top is golden brown.

Braised Shanks

Please, please, please stop throwing away those delicious venison shanks! Roasted in the oven and simmered in liquid, they make exceptional stocks and broths. But when braised osso bucco-style, the delicate, moist meat will impress even the most game-wary eater. The process takes a few hours, but it can be prepared a day or two in advance or frozen. A braised venison shank looks great on a plate nestled next to a mound of hot mashed potatoes or creamy polenta.

4 servings

INGREDIENTS

- 4 venison shanks
- salt and pepper
- flour
- ½ cup vegetable oil
- 2 cups onions, roughly chopped
- 2 cups carrots, roughly chopped
- 2 cups celery, roughly chopped
- 8 garlic cloves, minced
- 2 tablespoons tomato paste
- 2 cups beef, venison or game stock
- 1 cup dry white wine
- 1 sprig rosemary
- 1 or 2 sprigs thyme
- 3 bay leaves
- 1 teaspoon lemon zest
- 2 tablespoons parsley leaves, chopped

1. Preheat oven to 350 degrees. Dry venison shanks thoroughly with paper towels. Season liberally with salt and pepper, and dust with flour. Heat oil in a heavy-duty oven-safe pot (with lid, like a Dutch oven) over medium-high heat. Add venison, and brown evenly on all sides. Remove shanks from pot and reserve.

2. Add onions, carrots and celery to the pot, and lightly brown. Add garlic and tomato paste, and cook for 2 minutes. Add 1 cup of stock, and stir bottom of pot to loosen bits. Return shanks to the pot, add wine, rosemary, thyme and bay leaves. Liquid should always cover the shanks about halfway. Add stock to correct level, and reserve any extra to add later, if needed. Cover and place in the preheated oven for 2½ hours. Check after about 1½ hours, and see if any additional liquid is needed. Add more stock and/or wine if necessary.

3. When shanks are fork tender, transfer to plates or platter. Remove bay leaves. Spoon sauce and vegetables from pot over, and garnish with lemon zest and parsley.

Meatballs for the Masses

Many years ago, I owned a catering company, Silver Sage Caterers, with my buddy, Greg Cornell. I've since moved on to other, less demanding pursuits, but Greg's still cranking out some of the best chow in northern California. As any caterer knows, when preparing food for large groups, most of the grunt work has to be done well in advance. Large quantities of food are often produced in an assembly-line fashion. Making 100 meatballs goes much faster with three people than just one.

Suppose you have a big inventory of ground venison on hand. Or maybe you and your friends can combine their stock on hand to make a big pile of venison. That's when I'll throw out the idea that we join forces and produce enough tasty venison meatballs to have a big feed. And then again, you might just want to make the kitchen mess now and freeze the cooked meatballs in batches for future appetizers, or perhaps smothered in marinara sauce and Parmesan cheese.

48 meatballs, 10 to 12 servings

INGREDIENTS

- 3 pounds ground venison
- ¾ pound ground beef
- ¾ pound ground pork
- 3 eggs, lightly beaten
- 1½ tablespoons dried basil
- 1½ tablespoons dried parsley
- 1 tablespoon dried oregano
- 1 tablespoon garlic powder
- 1 tablespoon kosher salt
- 1 teaspoon red pepper flakes
- 1½ 10-ounce boxes frozen chopped spinach, thawed and drained
- 1½ cups Parmesan cheese, freshly grated
- 3 cups Japanese panko breadcrumbs
- pan spray

1. Preheat oven to 375 degrees. In a large bowl, combine all ingredients except breadcrumbs. Mix well (you're just going to have to use your hands). Add ¾ cup of the breadcrumbs, and mix well. Note: Make sure that the spinach is thoroughly drained. I press it between paper towels.

2. Divide the meatball mixture into 4 equal portions. Divide each portion in half. Form 6 equal-sized balls out of each of the 8 portions. Make sure to press the balls together firmly. Roll each ball in remaining breadcrumbs, and place on a lightly oiled baking pan. Spray meatballs lightly with pan spray, and place in the preheated oven for 20 minutes or until browned on the outside and just-cooked in the center.

Italian-Seasoned Venison Roast

Most folks don't think about eating venison meat cold, like any other cold cuts from the local deli. Marinated, seasoned and roasted to medium-rare, it's as good — no, better — than store-bought sliced meats. Sliced thin and piled high on toasted bread with cheese, onions, lettuce, tomato, mayo, pickles, now that's a sandwich! This recipe works best with roasts from the back half of a deer.

INGREDIENTS

- 1 3- to 5-pound venison roast
- ½ cup balsamic vinegar
- 8 to 10 garlic cloves, minced
- ⅔ cup onion, minced
- 3 tablespoons dried oregano
- 3 tablespoons dried basil
- 1 teaspoon Dijon mustard
- 2 teaspoons salt
- 1 teaspoon pepper
- ½ cup olive oil
- butcher string

1. Lay venison roast out on a work surface or cutting board. Starting at the bottom third of the roast, take a sharp knife and cut through the roast until the cut is about 1 inch from the next side. Do not cut all the way through the roast! Flop the roast open with the large side on the left and the smaller, thinner side on the right. Cut into the thicker side from the "hinge" side where you stopped cutting before. Cut until the knife is about 1 inch from the other side. Again, do not cut all the way through the roast. Press the meat down flat and place in a non-reactive container.

2. Whisk together vinegar and next 7 ingredients. While whisking, add oil in a thin stream until emulsified. Pour mixture over meat, and turn meat to coat evenly. Cover and refrigerate for 12 hours, turning occasionally. Remove from marinade, roll up roast, and tie up snugly with butcher string.

3. Preheat oven to 350 degrees. Place roast in a roasting pan, and cook in the preheated oven for 1½ hours or until roast reaches 135 degrees in the center for medium-rare. Cooking this roast well-done will result in a much drier, tougher piece of meat. Check internal temperature after 1 hour, and monitor internal temperature until it reaches desired doneness.

4. Allow roast to cool completely. It is best to slice after it has been refrigerated for at least 1 hour.

Guinness Oven Stew

I'm not a fan of drinking heavy, dark-colored beers, but the flavor a bold stout adds to a venison stew is incredible. As the beer reduces, it infuses the meat and broth with its hoppy, bittersweet flavor. This can be prepared in the oven or in a Dutch oven on the stovetop or campfire.

8 to 10 servings

INGREDIENTS

- 2 tablespoons butter
- 2 tablespoons flour
- 4 pounds (8 cups) venison stew meat, cut into 2-inch chunks
- salt and pepper
- 3 tablespoons vegetable oil
- 2 onions, roughly chopped
- 4 garlic cloves, minced
- 4 cups beef, venison or game stock
- 1 bottle Guinness Extra Stout (or other dark stout)
- 1 tablespoon light brown sugar
- 1 teaspoon dried thyme
- 1 teaspoon dried rosemary leaves
- 1 ounce bittersweet chocolate, chopped
- 2 bay leaves
- 5 carrots, peeled and roughly chopped
- 1½ pounds small red potatoes (creamers), cut in half

1. In a small skillet over medium heat, melt butter. Whisk flour into melted butter, and continue to cook while whisking constantly until mixture is light brown. Remove from heat, and allow to cool completely. This is a roux that will be used to thicken the stew much later.

2. Preheat oven to 350 degrees. Season stew meat liberally with salt and pepper. Heat 2 tablespoons oil in a large skillet over medium-high heat. Add meat and brown evenly. As meat is browned, transfer to a large, oven-safe pot.

3. Add remaining 1 tablespoon oil, onions, and garlic to skillet and cook until onions are lightly browned, about 5 minutes. Transfer to large pot with browned meat.

4. To pot, add stock, beer, brown sugar, thyme, rosemary, chocolate and bay leaves. Bring to a boil. Cover with tight-fitting lid or foil, and place in the preheated oven for 1½ hours. Add carrots and potatoes, and cook for another 30 minutes. Stew is done when meat is tender. If it doesn't break apart with moderate pressure, keep cooking.

5. Remove pot from oven, and place over on stovetop over medium heat. Whisk in reserved butter and flour mixture until liquid is thickened. If more liquid is needed for stew, add additional beer and/or stock before whisking in butter and flour mixture. Season to taste with salt and pepper.

Broiled Tenderloin

I don't soak my venison tenderloins in buttermilk, teriyaki sauce or anything else that is supposed to get rid of the gamey flavor. If your tenderloins taste gamey, it's your own darn fault. If you're going to cook a tenderloin in the oven, it should be broiled under high heat, not slow-cooked as with lesser, tough cuts of venison. High heat will give the meat a nice sear on the outside without overcooking the center.

As a reminder, tenderloins are the flat muscles located along the inside of the spine. Outside are the larger loins, or backstraps. Tenderloins are so named because they really don't do much work. They are just along for the ride and don't get much of a workout, so they remain soft and tender. Ideally, this dish should be prepared in a preheated cast iron skillet. Place the skillet under the broiler for 5 minutes to get it hot, and then immediately place the meat in the skillet and return it to the broiler. It's also very important to let the tenderloin sit at room temperature for 15 to 20 minutes before cooking so that the inside temperature is about the same as the outside. As always, let the meat rest for a few minutes after removing from the hot skillet.

4 servings

INGREDIENTS

- 1 or 2 venison tenderloins, depending on size
- 3 tablespoons olive oil
- ¼ teaspoon salt
- 1 tablespoon cracked black pepper
- 2 cloves garlic, minced
- ¼ cup red wine vinegar
- 1 teaspoon Dijon mustard
- 1 onion, peeled and quartered
- 2 tablespoons butter

1. Place tenderloins, olive oil, salt, pepper, garlic, vinegar, mustard and onion in a zipper-lock bag. Shake bag to combine ingredients. Refrigerate for 1 to 4 hours.

2. Remove bag from refrigerator, and leave at room temperature for 15 to 20 minutes. Remove meat and onion from bag. Discard marinade. Place meat and onion in a preheated heavy-duty, oven-safe skillet (like cast iron), and place immediately under a preheated broiler, about 5 to 6 inches from the heat source. Broil for 4 to 5 minutes, then remove skillet from broiler. Transfer meat to a plate or cutting board, and let rest for a few minutes. Meanwhile, whisk butter into skillet.

3. To serve, slice tenderloin, and arrange on plates or platter with onion. Drizzle butter sauce over.

Sweet-Hot Oven Jerky

Any jerky should be used as only as an outline. If you have any level of kitchen sense, you'll figure out how to make the next batch even better. The trouble with my own jerky recipes is that I often make a really good batch only to realize that during the process, I must have gotten distracted and didn't pay much attention to what I was adding to the marinade or rub. My friends will ask, "What did you do to make this jerky taste so good?" and I'll have to make something up. So, keep a scratch pad handy as you create your own signature venison jerky.

It's always best to keep jerky refrigerated or, if you don't plan on eating it for a couple of weeks or more, frozen. I vacuum-pack mine in small batches, stick them in the freezer and throw a bag or two into my pack when I'm headed to the woods or water. Don't worry about keeping it refrigerated for a day or two. They'll be fine in your gear bag.

For 2 pounds of meat

INGREDIENTS

- 1 cup soy sauce
- ¼ cup Worcestershire sauce
- ¼ cup Kosher salt
- ¼ cup brown sugar
- 1 tablespoon freshly ground black pepper
- 1 tablespoon garlic powder
- 1 teaspoon cayenne pepper

1. Remove gristle and silver skin from meat. Slice as thinly as possible. If you prefer a chewier jerky, slice the meat along the grain. For more tender jerky, cut across the grain. If needed, lightly pound meat until it is of even thickness. Combine soy sauce and Worcestershire sauce in a medium bowl, add sliced meat, and toss to coat evenly. Cover and refrigerate for 12 to 24 hours. Remove meat from marinade, and pat dry.

2. Combine Kosher salt with remaining ingredients. Coat meat evenly, and stack sliced game one on top of the other. Wrap with plastic wrap and refrigerate for 12 hours.

3. Dry meat in a single layer on racks in a 160-degree oven with the door open about ½ inch to allow moisture to escape. If your oven does not have tab that keeps the door open, use a ball of foil, and place between the door and the oven. Average drying time is 4 hours, depending on meat thickness.

chapter 7

Stovetop

Every home chef appreciates a one-pan meal that's easy to prepare and cooks in just a few minutes. Blackened, pan-seared, pan-fried, deep-fried or sautéed, all you need is a good, sharp knife, a handful of ingredients and a big skillet to create a sensational meal.

I do most of my cooking on a stovetop. I've done hundreds of demonstrations, preparing as many as 20 dishes in a couple of hours, using only a portable burner and a pile of skillets. The key is to have all ingredients prepped and arranged in the order that they will be added to the skillet or pot. Shortly before dinner time, fire up the pan, start cooking, and you're usually done in 10 minutes or so.

My skillet of choice is seasoned cast iron. Because I'm an admitted cookware abuser, I can't justify high-dollar pots and pans that require special care. Cast iron can be left outside for a year and still brought back to life. Properly seasoned and with minimal care, cast iron actually gets better with age.

Maple Breakfast Sausage with Buttery Red Eye Gravy

It's been my experience that most folks won't bother giving a sausage recipe a second look. They think it requires special equipment and a chemistry degree. Grinders, cures and casings — and, really, what are those casings made of anyway? This breakfast sausage recipe is as simple as making venison burgers. Nothing more than a knife and a pair of hands is required. Uncooked sausages can be frozen for a year or so.

Makes about 5 pounds

INGREDIENTS

- 8 cups (4 pounds) ground venison
- 2 cups (1 pound) ground pork
- 2 tablespoons kosher salt
- 2 tablespoons rubbed (ground) sage, or 1 tablespoon fresh minced sage leaves
- 1 tablespoon ground black pepper
- 1 tablespoon red pepper flakes
- 2 tablespoons freshly squeezed lemon juice
- ½ cup real maple syrup

BUTTERY RED EYE GRAVY

- Makes ½ cup
- 4 strips bacon
- ½ cup strong-brewed coffee
- ¼ cup beef or venison broth
- 3 tablespoons chilled butter
- freshly ground black pepper
- pinch salt

1. In a large bowl, combine all sausage ingredients, and mix well. Divide into four equal portions. Each of the four portions will make about 6 3-ounce patties. You can make each portion into individual patties and freeze, or freeze the portions in bulk and make the patties at a later date. Or you can make a big pile of delicious sausages and invite family and friends over for breakfast.

2. Form sausage mixture into patties, and press firmly to help hold them together while cooking. Place sausages into a lightly oiled skillet over medium heat. Brown evenly on both sides until just cooked but not overcooked. Remove sausages from pan, and keep warm.

3. Add bacon to pan, and cook until lightly browned. Remove bacon, and leave grease in pan. Increase heat to medium-high and add coffee and venison broth. Stir to remove bits stuck to pan. Cook until liquid is reduced by ½. Remove from heat, and whisk butter into pan until emulsified. Whisk in pepper and salt. Arrange sausages on plates or a platter, and spoon sauce over.

Freezer tip: If you choose to freeze uncooked sausage patties, place them on a lightly greased baking sheet, and place in the freezer until completely frozen. Place a small square of wax pepper between patties, and freeze with a vacuum packaging unit or in freezer-safe zipper-lock bags.

Breakfast Steak, Egg and Cheesy Cat Head Biscuit Sandwich

It's a Southern thing, or "thang." From the Mississippi Delta to the Appalachians of Virginia, I've been served cat head biscuits in various forms, and they've all been exceptionally good. Some are light and flaky, others a bit on the heavy side. The "cat head" name comes from the irregular shape of the oversized biscuits. I like mine with a little spicy mustard.

Four servings, eight biscuits

INGREDIENTS

- 4 4-ounce venison cube steaks
- 2 tablespoons olive oil
- salt and pepper

- 1 tablespoon butter
- 4 large eggs
- 4 thin slices tomato

CHEESY CAT HEAD BISCUITS

- 2 cups flour
- 1 tablespoon baking powder
- ½ teaspoon baking soda
- ½ teaspoon salt
- ⅓ cup shortening
- 1½ tablespoons butter
- ⅔ cup buttermilk
- 1 cup sharp cheddar cheese, grated

1. Prepare biscuits. Preheat oven to 450 degrees. Sift flour, baking powder, baking soda and salt into a large mixing bowl, and mix well. Using a pastry cutter or two knives, cut in shortening and butter until it has the texture of coarse cornmeal. Blend buttermilk into flour mixture until evenly moist. Add cheese, and work into mixture. Turn dough mixture out onto a lightly floured surface, and knead until dough is even but not overworked. The less the dough is kneaded, the flakier the biscuits when cooked.

2. Break the dough into 8 relatively equal portions, and lightly form into balls, pressing down until the balls are about ½ inch thick. Place onto a lightly greased baking sheet, at least 1 inch apart, and place into the preheated oven. Bake 10 to 15 minutes or until golden brown. Allow biscuits to cool for 5 minutes, and then split.

3. Heat olive oil in a large skillet over medium-high heat. Season venison with salt and pepper, and brown in skillet on both sides. Transfer to a plate or pan, and keep warm. Return skillet to stove, melt butter and add eggs to pan. Cook until yolks are done as per your preference — sunny side up, medium or other.

4. For each biscuit, place tomato slice on the bottom half, top with venison, egg and biscuit top. Of course, you'll have a few extra biscuits, just in case.

Venison and Mushroom Ragout on Soft Parmesan Polenta

A ragout is a stew with French roots that's rich, hearty and pairs slow-cooked meats with vegetables or beans. I've mixed in a pile of mushrooms and served it on top of soft, cheesy polenta. For my Southern friends, feel free to substitute cheese grits for the polenta. If you're long on venison stew meat, double the recipe, and freeze some for later.

6 servings

INGREDIENTS

- 6 strips smoky bacon, diced
- 1 tablespoon olive oil
- 2 tablespoons butter
- 4 cups venison stew meat, cut into 2-inch chunks
- salt and pepper
- 1½ cups yellow onion, finely diced
- 1½ cups carrots, finely diced
- 1½ cups celery, finely diced
- 2 tablespoons flour
- 3 cups beef stock or game stock
- ¼ cup brandy
- 3 tablespoons tomato paste
- 2 teaspoons Italian seasoning
- 3 cups small mushrooms, ends trimmed
- salt and pepper

PARMESAN POLENTA

- 4 cups chicken broth
- 2 cups half and half
- 2 tablespoons butter
- 1½ cups yellow polenta or cornmeal
- 1 cup Parmesan cheese, grated or shredded (not the stuff in the green can)
- salt

1. In a large heavy-duty stock pot or Dutch oven over medium-high heat, add bacon, and lightly brown. Add oil and butter, and heat until butter is melted. Add meat, and brown evenly. While browning, season meat with salt and pepper. Stir in onion, carrots and celery, and cook until onions are translucent. Sprinkle flour over meat and vegetables while stirring. Cook for 5 minutes, stirring often.

2. Stir in beef or game stock, brandy, tomato paste and Italian seasoning. Bring to a boil, then reduce heat to low, and simmer for 1½ to 2 hours or until meat is tender. If meat does not break apart with minimal finger pressure, keep cooking. If necessary, add additional stock to just below the top of the meat and vegetables. Add mushrooms and cook for 5 to 7 minutes more.

3. To prepare polenta, heat chicken broth and half-and-half to a boil in a large saucepan. Stir in butter. Stir in polenta or cornmeal, a little at a time. Continue to stir until mixture is hot and bubbly. Reduce heat to low, and cook for 20 to 25 minutes, stirring frequently. Stir in cheese, and season to taste with salt.

4. To serve, spoon polenta into large bowls and spoon ragout over.

Blackened Backstrap

The key to blackening is to use a heavy skillet, preferably cast iron, and screaming-hot heat. Restaurants that serve blackened meats and fish keep a white-hot skillet over a burner at all times. I highly recommend that you open the doors and windows and provide as much ventilation as possible. Done properly, there's plenty of smoke. Adding insult to smoke, when you blacken a hunk of meat, you're actually burning the peppery spices that coat the outside. Inhaling hot, peppery smoke might cause watery eyes and a burning throat. If you have a high-BTU outside burner and a well-seasoned cast-iron skillet, that's ideal. If I haven't scared you off, proceed with caution.

4 servings

INGREDIENTS

- 4 8-ounce backstrap steaks, butterflied
- 2 tablespoons melted butter

BLACKENING SPICE RUB

- 2 tablespoons paprika
- 1 tablespoon each ground oregano, ground thyme and cayenne pepper
- 1 teaspoon each ground black pepper, ground white pepper, garlic powder and onion powder
- 8 thick slices tomato
- 4 tablespoons sour cream
- 1 teaspoon fresh parsley leaves, minced

1. Coat steaks with melted butter. Combine rub ingredients, and coat meat evenly. Save extra spice mix for blackening fish, game, beef or pork at a later date.

2. Heat a cast-iron skillet over high heat for at least 20 minutes. Place steaks in pan, and cook about 3 minutes per side for medium-rare.

Note: Provide adequate ventilation, and do not breathe smoke or fumes.

3. Place two tomato slices on each plate. Set meat on tomato. Top with a tablespoon of sour cream, and sprinkle parsley over.

Cubed Steaks with Black Pepper and Tomato Sauce

If you have your animals processed by a pro, there's a good chance you'll end up with a fair amount of cube steaks. Tougher cuts are run through a tenderizer, or "cuber." If you process several of your own deer, consider a hand-operated or electric home cuber. They're pretty handy.

4 servings

INGREDIENTS

- 4 venison cubed steaks
- 3 tablespoons flour
- ½ teaspoon salt
- ¼ teaspoon pepper
- 3 eggs
- 2 tablespoons milk
- ½ cup saltine crackers, crushed
- ⅓ cup Parmesan cheese, grated
- peanut, canola or vegetable oil
- 1 teaspoon dried basil leaves
- 3 tablespoons vegetable oil
- 4 medium tomatoes, quartered and tossed lightly to dislodge seeds
- 1 cup onion, diced
- 3 garlic cloves, minced
- 1 tablespoon cracked black pepper
- 1 teaspoon dried oregano leaves
- 1 teaspoon sugar
- 4 slices mozzarella cheese

1. Preheat oven to 400 degrees. In a shallow bowl, combine flour, salt and pepper. In another bowl, beat together eggs and milk. In another shallow bowl, combine cracker crumbs, Parmesan cheese and basil.

2. Dry cubed steaks thoroughly with paper or clean cloth towels. Dunk dried steaks in the flour mixture, then the egg mixture, then the cracker mixture, pressing down into the cracker mixture to evenly coat both sides.

3. Heat about ½ inch of oil in a large skillet over medium-high heat. Add coated steaks, and brown evenly on both sides. Remove from pan, then drain on paper towels and place in a lightly greased baking dish.

4. Combine tomato, onion, garlic, pepper, oregano and sugar in a medium bowl. After steaks are browned, spoon tomato mixture over each, and place in oven for 10 minutes. Top each with a slice of cheese, and return to oven until cheese is melted.

Mustard-Fried Cubed Steaks with Chimichurri Sauce

I'm always on the hunt for new and interesting mustard blends. Dijon, whole grain, blended with wine, herbs and spices — they're all great accompaniments for a seared piece of deer meat, provided you like mustard. If mustard doesn't honk your horns, you've probably already moved on to another recipe.

Chimichurri sauce has its garlicky roots in Argentina, and is a great accompaniment for venison, beef, pork or chicken. You'll have a little left over that can be stored for a week or two in the refrigerator.

4 servings

INGREDIENTS

- 1 cup Dijon mustard
- 1 cup dry white wine
- 4 to 8 10-ounce venison cubed steaks
- 2 cups flour
- ½ teaspoon salt
- ¼ teaspoon pepper
- oil for frying

CHIMICHURRI SAUCE

- 1 cup fresh Italian parsley, packed
- 2 tablespoons fresh oregano leaves
- 5 cloves garlic
- ⅓ cup red wine vinegar
- ¾ teaspoon red pepper flakes
- ½ teaspoon salt
- ½ cup extra virgin olive oil

1. Prepare Chimichurri sauce. Place all ingredients except olive oil in a food processor, and pulse to blend. In between pulses, scrape sides of the processor bowl down. Transfer to a medium bowl, and whisk in olive oil.

2. In a zipper-lock bag, combine the mustard and wine. Add steaks, and toss to mix well. Close bag, and refrigerate for 2 to 4 hours. Remove steaks from marinade, and pat dry.

3. Combine flour, salt and pepper in a shallow bowl. Heat about ¼ inch of oil in a large skillet over medium-high heat. Dust steaks with flour mixture, and fry in hot oil until golden brown. Drain on paper towels. Serve with a dollop of Chimichurri sauce.

Cheesesteak

In the tradition of the Philly cheesesteak sandwich, this recipe is a quickie that'll fool some of your friends who claim that they don't like the taste of venison. Just don't tell them it's deer meat until after the first few bites. The meat is sliced very thin, so be careful when cooking. It only tastes a minute or two to cook it.

4 servings

INGREDIENTS

- 3 cups trimmed venison steak
- salt and pepper
- 2 tablespoons olive oil
- 1 large yellow onion, thinly sliced
- 1 green bell pepper, thinly sliced
- 3 garlic cloves, minced
- 2 cups mushrooms, thinly sliced
- dash Tabasco
- 8 slices provolone cheese
- 4 Italian rolls, split

1. Place venison in a freezer for an hour or so until the meat is almost frozen. Using a sharp, thin-bladed knife, slice the meat as thinly as possible. Allow to thaw completely, wrap with paper towels to absorb blood, and season liberally with salt and pepper.

2. Heat olive oil in a large, heavy skillet or griddle over medium-high heat. Add onions, pepper and garlic. Cook until onions are lightly browned. Add mushrooms, and sauté with onions and peppers until soft.

3. Move vegetables to one side of the skillet, and add sliced venison. Cook meat until lightly brown, but not overcooked. Season with a dash or two of Tabasco.

4. Mound meat into 4 rectangular piles, about the size of the Italian rolls. Top with equal portions of the vegetable mixture. Top with 2 slices of cheese for each mound until cheese melts.

5. Using two spatulas, scoop up each portion of meat and vegetables, and place in Italian rolls.

Deer Scaloppine

There are many versions of the classic Italian scaloppine, which consists of thinly sliced meat, usually veal or chicken, that has been floured and sauteed with wine, chicken, beef or veal stock and a handful of other ingredients. The key is to watch the cooking time. Sliced thinly, your venison will overcook in a heartbeat.

4 servings

INGREDIENTS

- 2 pounds venison, trimmed of all silver skin and sinew
- salt and coarsely ground black pepper
- ⅔ cup flour
- 6 tablespoons butter, divided in half
- 2 tablespoons olive oil
- 2 tablespoons lemon juice, preferably freshly squeezed
- 3 cloves garlic, minced
- ¼ cup dry red wine
- ¼ cup beef, veal or venison broth
- 2 cups mushrooms, thinly sliced
- 1 tablespoon capers, rinsed and drained
- 1 teaspoon Italian seasoning (or substitute fresh herbs)
- 1 cup tomato, seeded, peeled and diced
- warm, cooked pasta
- shredded Parmesan cheese

1. Cut meat into 1- to 2-inch pieces. Place inside a zipper-lock bag or between wax paper sheets, and pound lightly until each piece is about ⅛ inch thick. Season with salt and pepper. Place flour in a shallow dish, and dredge seasoned meat lightly in flour.

2. Heat half of the butter with the olive oil in a large skillet over medium-high heat. Add venison medallions, a few pieces at a time, browning evenly on both sides — about 1 minute per side. When cooked, transfer to a plate with paper towels to drain. Cover with foil, and keep warm.

3. When all meat is browned, add lemon juice, garlic, wine and broth to pan. Stir to scrape bits, and add mushroom, capers and Italian seasoning. Cook until liquid is reduced to ⅓ cup. Stir in remaining butter until melted. Stir in tomato.

4. Mound pasta on plates, arrange cooked venison over pasta, and spoon sauce over. Top with Parmesan cheese.

Semi-Stroganoff

INGREDIENTS

- 2 pounds venison, carefully trimmed and sliced thinly across the grain into strips
- 2 tablespoons olive oil
- salt and pepper
- ¾ cup butter
- 1 large yellow onion, diced
- 4 cups mushrooms, quartered
- 5 garlic cloves, minced
- 1 teaspoon Worcestershire sauce
- ¾ cup game or beef stock
- 2 fresh sage leaves, minced (or sub pinch dried sage leaves)
- ⅓ cup sour cream
- 4 cups wide noodles, cooked and warm
- 2 tablespoons red bell pepper, finely diced
- ½ cup blue cheese crumbles
- minced parsley

1. Heat oil in a large skillet over medium-high heat. Season meat with salt and pepper, and brown evenly, but not past medium-rare.

2. Remove meat, and transfer to a bowl. Melt butter in pan, and add onions. Cook for 5 minutes. Add mushroms. Cook for 4 minutes more. Add garlic, Worcestershire, broth and sage leaves. Reduce heat to low, and simmer, uncovered, until liquid is reduced to about ½ cup.

3. Stir in sour cream, and heat while stirring often, for 3 to 4 minutes or until sauce is bubbly.

4. Return venison to pan to warm.

5. Mound noodles on plates, top with stroganoff mixture, and top with red bell pepper, blue cheese crumbles and parsley.

So You Don't Like Venison?

While traveling the countryside the past couple of decades sharing my personal brand of wild-game cooking, I've run across many people who just don't like venison. If I had to guess what went wrong, somebody served them an overcooked "gamey" piece of improperly prepared deer meat. Venison has about five times less fat than beef, so it's not nearly as forgiving as a marbled beef ribeye. Fat also equals flavor and juiciness. If you overcook a venison steak, it will be dry and livery.

This is my go-to recipe when faced with the challenge of convincing people that if their venison doesn't taste good, don't blame the deer. I cook the meat rare to medium-rare and cover it with some of the dark, rich sauce, just in case they pale at the sight of red, not overcooked, grayish meat.

If you have tenderloins or backstrap medallions, that will increase your chances of impressing those who are game-shy. Trimmed hindquarter steaks can be tenderized and sliced across the grain before serving, but please don't overcook them. If you are accustomed to eating your red meats on the well-done side, please, just once, try it cooked medium-rare.

4 servings

INGREDIENTS

- 2 pounds trimmed venison medallions, about 4 inches wide by ½ inch thick
- salt and pepper
- 2 tablespoons olive oil
- ½ teaspoon fresh rosemary leaves, minced
- 2 cloves garlic, minced
- ¼ cup balsamic vinegar
- 1 tablespoon plum preserves
- 3 tablespoons chilled butter, cut into pieces
- ¾ cup fresh berries, any kind
- ¼ cup blue cheese crumbles (optional, if you like blue cheese)

1. Season meat evenly with salt and pepper. Heat olive oil in a large skillet over medium-high heat. Add meat and brown, about 1 to 2 minutes each side, but not past rare. Add rosemary, garlic, balsamic vinegar and plum preserves. Remove meat after 1 minute and keep warm.

2. Reduce liquid to a few tablespoons. Whisk in chilled butter until melted. Immediately remove pan from heat, and stir in berries. Arrange medallions on plates, spoon sauce over and, if desired, top with blue cheese crumbles.

Sloppy Josés

This recipe is a bit of a throwback to my school days, when my mother would blend canned Manwich sauce with cooked ground beef. Truth be told, I got really tired of eating sloppy joes. I'm pretty sure that I went 25 years or so before eating another one after high school. That is, until I helped make a giant batch of venison sloppy joes for a Sportsman Channel Hunt, Fish, Feed event. Sportsman Channel, along with a great group of volunteers, turns donated fish and game into healthy meals for the hungry and homeless across the United States. The real credit goes to those folks who work in the shelters across the county, feeding hundreds, sometimes thousands, of needy people every day.

This is my own spiced-up version of a sloppy joe. They say your taste buds get worn out with age. I believe that's true.

6 servings

INGREDIENTS

- 2 tablespoons vegetable oil
- 1 medium onion, diced
- 1 bell pepper, diced
- 1 jalapeño pepper, seeded and minced
- 1 cup celery, finely diced
- 1 pound ground venison
- $\frac{1}{3}$ pound ground beef — 20 percent fat
- 1 tablespoon garlic powder
- 1 teaspoon dried oregano leaves
- 1 teaspoon chili powder
- $\frac{1}{2}$ teaspoon ground cumin
- $\frac{2}{3}$ cup tomato salsa
- 1 tablespoon freshly squeezed lime juice
- 3 tablespoons light brown sugar
- 2 tablespoons tequila (optional)
- $\frac{1}{4}$ cup fresh cilantro leaves, chopped
- salt and pepper to taste
- burger buns or large flour tortillas

1. Heat oil over medium heat in a large skillet. Add onion, peppers and celery, and cook until onions are translucent.

2. Mix venison and beef together, and add to pan, breaking apart as it cooks. When browned, stir in garlic powder, oregano, chili powder, cumin, salsa, lime juice, brown sugar, tequila and brown sugar. Reduce heat to low, and simmer for 20 to 25 minutes. Stir in cilantro, and season to taste with salt and pepper.

3. Spoon meat into buns or tortillas, and serve.

Venison Manicotti

This is a favorite way to use braised, shredded meat from venison neck and shoulder roasts. You can also substitute browned ground meat.

6 servings

INGREDIENTS

- 4 tablespoons olive oil
- 1 medium onion, coarsely chopped
- 4 garlic cloves, minced
- 1 pound cooked shredded venison meat
- salt and pepper
- 1 15-ounce container whole-milk ricotta
- 3 cups shredded mozzarella cheese
- 1 cup shredded Parmesan cheese
- 1 teaspoon Italian seasoning
- 3 cups marinara sauce
- 1 8-ounce package manicotti

1. Preheat oven to 350 degrees. Heat 1 tablespoon oil in a skillet over medium heat. Add onion and garlic, and cook for 3 to 4 minutes. Transfer to a large bowl, and combine with venison. Season with salt and pepper.

2. In another bowl, combine ricotta and half of the mozzarella and Parmesan cheeses. Add Italian seasoning. Combine cheese mixture with meat mixture, and stir to blend.

3. Cook manicotti in a large pot of boiling salted water for 4 to 6 minutes. Lightly coat a baking sheet with 1 tablespoon oil. When cooked, use a slotted spoon to transfer manicotti to the oiled baking sheet, and allow to cool.

4. Coat a 13-by-9-by-2-inch baking dish with remaining 2 tablespoons oil. Spread half of the marinara sauce over the bottom of the pan. Spoon meat and cheese mixture into cooled manicotti tubes, and arrange in a single layer in the dish. Spoon remaining sauce over, and top with remaining cheeses.

5. Bake uncovered in a preheated 350-degree oven until heated throughout and bubbly, about 30 minutes. Let stand for 5 minutes before serving (this allows mixture to set up).

Shrooms Times Two

Too many home game chefs have turned to the slow-cooker and a can of cream of mushroom soup to turn their venison into something that tastes like, well, cream of mushroom soup. I understand that it's easy and edible, but it's just not for me. This recipe combines a mushroomy crusted venison steak with a creamy mushroom sauce. If there is an Asian market nearby, that's your best resource for dried mushrooms. Those dried shrooms found in small packages in grocery stores can be a bit pricey.

4 servings

INGREDIENTS

- 1½ cups dried shiitake, porcini or crimini mushrooms
- 1 tablespoon fresh sage leaves, minced
- 4 8- to 10-ounce venison steaks
- salt and pepper
- 2 tablespoons Dijon mustard
- 2 tablespoons olive oil
- 1 tablespoon fresh parsley leaves, minced
- pinch or two paprika

MUSHROOM SAUCE

- 2 tablespoons butter
- 2 tablespoons flour
- ½ cup chicken broth
- ¼ cup dry white wine
- ¼ cup whipping cream
- 1 teaspoon Worcestershire sauce
- dash Tabasco
- 2 green onions, white and green part, diced
- 2 garlic cloves, minced
- 2 cups fresh mushrooms, chopped
- salt and pepper to taste

1. Prepare mushroom sauce. Melt butter in a medium saucepan over medium heat. Stir in flour, and cook while stirring until butter/flour mixture is smooth and beige in color, about 3 to 5 minutes. Stir in chicken broth, a little at a time, until incorporated. Stir in wine and cream until smooth. Add remaining sauce ingredients, and simmer for 10 to 12 minutes, stirring often. Season to taste with salt and pepper.

2. Place mushrooms and sage in a food processor, and pulse until it turns to powder. Season medallions with salt and pepper, then coat with mustard. Dust steaks with mushroom and sage powder. Heat oil in a large skillet over medium-high heat, add venison and sear on both sides until medium-rare. To serve, spoon sauce on to plates, arrange steaks over sauce, and garnish with parsley and paprika.

Pan-Seared Tenderloin with Zinfandel Sauce

I rarely recommend using a specific type of wine in a recipe. You've undoubtedly heard from the TV chefs that, "You shouldn't cook with a wine you wouldn't drink." Don't believe it. If you take a peek into the kitchens of most dinner houses, you'll see cooks using very generic red and white wines for cooking. Partial bottles left over from wine-by-the-glass selections at the bar and big 18-liter spigoted boxes of Chablis and Burgundy are the rule, not the exception.

I prefer to cook with unflavored, generic wines and save my money on the wine I drink. This recipe is one of a few exceptions. A decent, peppery zinfandel is ideal as a finisher to the dish, added just before serving so that the flavor of the wine remains. If you're short on zinfandel, use any other bold, unflavored red wine.

4 servings

INGREDIENTS

- 1 or 2 venison tenderloins, cut into serving-sized pieces
- salt and pepper
- 1 tablespoon olive oil
- 2 cups beef or venison stock
- 1 teaspoon fresh rosemary leaves, minced
- 1 clove garlic, minced
- ½ teaspoon freshly ground black pepper
- 1 cup zinfandel
- 4 tablespoons chilled butter, cut into 6 to 8 pieces

1. Season venison with salt and pepper. Heat olive oil in a large skillet over medium-high heat. Add venison and cook until rare to medium-rare, about 4 to 5 minutes to brown both sides. Remove meat from pan, and keep warm.

2. Add stock, rosemary, garlic and pepper to pan. Stir to remove bits. Heat to a boil, then reduce heat and simmer until liquid is reduced to about 3 tablespoons. Add wine, and reduce liquid to about ¼ cup. Return venison to pan to warm through to serving temperature.

3. Arrange venison on plates. Remove pan from heat, and whisk in butter pieces, a few at a time, until incorporated into the sauce. Spoon sauce over venison.

Deer Diane

Picture the waiter with the fancy outfit and the snotty attitude preparing a flaming steak Diane tableside at a white tablecloth restaurant. Now imagine the same guy screaming as he runs away with his mustache on fire. Know why? He wasn't paying attention when he cooked with brandy and an open flame. Follow the directions carefully. That includes removing the pan from anywhere near the stove when you add the remaining ingredients, especially brandy.

4 servings

INGREDIENTS

- 1½ pounds (about 3 cups) venison tenderloin or backstrap
- salt and pepper
- 1 onion, finely chopped
- 2 cloves garlic, minced
- 2 tablespoons butter
- 2 tablespoons Worcestershire sauce
- ¼ cup brandy
- ¼ cup beef or venison stock
- 1 teaspoon Dijon mustard
- 3 cups mushrooms, quartered
- ¼ cup heavy (whipping) cream
- 2 tablespoons fresh parsley, minced

1. Place venison on a flat surface. Cut into 2-inch chunks. Place chunks, a few at a time, between wax paper sheets and lightly pound with a mallet or heavy skillet until meat is about ¼ inch thick. Season meat with salt and pepper.

2. Melt butter over medium heat in a large skillet. Add onion, and cook until translucent, about 4 to 5 minutes. Add venison, and cook on both sides until rare. Remove venison from pan, and set aside.

3. Remove pan from heat and away from any open flame or heat source. In a small bowl, combine Worcestershire sauce, brandy, stock and mustard, and stir into pan. Return pan to the heat, add mushrooms, and cook until mushrooms are soft and just cooked. Stir in heavy cream, and bring to a boil, stirring to transform sauce into a smooth mixture. Cook until sauce thickens. Season to taste with salt and pepper.

4. Return meat to pan to warm, about 1 minute. Spoon meat and sauce onto plates, and top with fresh parsley.

Sausage with Rustic Tomato Sauce

In the summertime, when "real" homegrown tomatoes are available, this is one of my favorite recipes. During the tomato offseason, I'll usually prepare this dish with canned tomatoes rather than grocery store tomatoes. Then I won't whine about the lack of flavor from the so-called "vine-ripened" store-bought tomatoes as compared to the real deals. Who do they think they're fooling? Although this recipe is a main-course serving, you can also serve it without the pasta as an appetizer course.

4 servings

INGREDIENTS

- 4 large venison sausages
- 3 tablespoons extra-virgin olive oil
- 1 onion, diced
- 1 cup carrots, peeled and thinly sliced
- 4 cloves garlic, thinly sliced
- 3 cups tomatoes, roughly chopped
- 1 tablespoon balsamic vinegar
- pinch sugar
- pinch or two red pepper flakes
- ½ cup kalamata olives, seeded and chopped
- 2 cups fresh basil leaves, chopped
- 1 tablespoon fresh oregano leaves, minced
- salt and pepper to taste
- 6 cups warm, cooked pasta – any variety
- 2 tablespoons melted butter

1. Heat 1 tablespoon olive oil in a large skillet over medium heat. Add sausages, and brown evenly, about 6 to 7 minutes. Add remaining 2 tablespoons olive oil, onion and carrots. Sauté for 4 to 5 minutes. Add garlic, and sauté 2 minutes more. Add tomatoes, vinegar, sugar, pepper flakes, olives, basil and oregano, and cook for 3 minutes. Season to taste with salt and pepper.

2. Toss pasta with butter, and mound on plates. Top with a sausage, and spoon tomato mixture over.

Spicy Black Bean Stir-Fry

Not to be confused with a Southwestern black bean dish, this recipe is a somewhat spicy version of a traditional Asian stir-fry. As with any stir-fry, you'll spend more time prepping than cooking. Just make sure that all of your ingredients are chopped and ready to go before you fire up the wok or skillet. The meat needs to be cooked quickly and then removed from the pan to avoid overcooking. If "spicy" doesn't work for you, just leave out the Asian hot sauce, and it will just be a bit peppery.

4 servings

INGREDIENTS

- 3 cups venison backstrap, tenderloin or well-trimmed hindquarter steaks
- 1 teaspoon freshly ground black pepper
- 2 tablespoons peanut oil
- 1 cup bell pepper, any color, thinly sliced
- 3 garlic cloves, minced
- 1½ cups beef broth
- 2 cups cooked black beans (canned OK)
- 3 tablespoons low-sodium soy sauce
- 1 teaspoon hoisin sauce
- 1 tablespoon Sriracha or any Asian chili-garlic sauce
- ¼ teaspoon sesame oil
- 3 tablespoons rice vinegar
- 2 tablespoons plum preserves
- 3 green onions, chopped
- 1 tablespoon pickled ginger, minced
- 2 teaspoons cornstarch mixed with 2 teaspoons cold water
- 4 cups warm cooked rice

1. Lightly pound the venison with a mallet or heavy skillet until meat is of even thickness, about ¼ inch thick. Cut venison across the grain into slices. The shape of the slices isn't important, just the thickness. Thin is better, and more tender when cooked, than thick. Toss sliced meat with pepper and 1 tablespoon of the peanut oil. Heat remaining oil in a wok or large skillet over medium-high heat, add meat and cook for 2 to 3 minutes, but meat should still be rare to medium-rare. Remove meat from pan, and set aside.

2. Add bell pepper and garlic, and cook for 3 minutes. Add beef broth, and bring to a boil. Stir in black beans and remaining ingredients except cornstarch mixture and rice. Cook for 5 minutes to blend flavors. Return cooked venison to pan, stir in cornstarch mixture, and heat until thickened. Serve over rice.

chapter 8

Smoking

This is not a step-by-step manual on how to smoke venison. I've made a few assumptions, probably not entirely correct. I'm assuming that you own a refrigerator and your refrigerator has a freezer. If you shoot a fair amount of game, you probably also have a separate freezer for storage. The potential for spoilage scares some people away from buying a smoker. There's no need to concern yourself with food spoilage unless you plan on leaving a hunk of smoked meat on the hood of your truck for a day or so in the middle of summer. You smoke it, and then you eat it or freeze it for later.

Smoking and smoke-cooking are more popular than ever. Home grill units are commonly equipped with a separate smoke box for indirect, low-temperature smoking and smoke cooking. If all you own is a propane-fueled grill, well, you're just not going to have much luck smoking venison. I've tried using pans that hold smoke chips, smoke canisters and other devices designed to turn a propane grill into a smoker, but I haven't had much success. You'll get a little smoke flavor but not much more.

Any charcoal or wood-fired grill can be used as a smoker. Keep the temperature low and the meat as far away from the heat source as possible. You can't rush smoking meat. It takes time for the smoke to penetrate the outside of the meat, giving you the reddish "smoke ring" around the edges.

If you don't own a reliable meat thermometer, put this cookbook down, and go get one. Professional chefs use them, barbecue competitors use them, and I use them. Because smoking big hunks of venison can take several hours, you might consider buying a remote thermometer that comes with a probe and wireless receiver. At any time, you can check the internal temperature of your roast from the comfort of your couch. It'll even let you know when it's done. Technology meets one of the oldest cooking methods known to man.

Brines and Rubs

A brine is just a salty solution that will enhance and preserve the flavor of cooked meat. A proper brine will replace venison blood with brine. It's been my experience that brine tastes better than any wild-game blood. The blood-colored juice that runs out of a medium-rare piece of meat is why some folks prefer to cook it until it's tough and leathery. Hey, it might taste muttony, but at least it's not bloody. Me, I'm OK with a little juice on the plate, but if your goal is to get someone to try their venison less-cooked and still tender, brining it first to remove the blood will vastly improve the chance that they'll eat it.

Note that the brine recipe below specifies kosher salt. Kosher salt is a larger-grained salt than regular table salt. There is more air space between grains, making it less dense than finer-ground salt. If all you have on hand is table salt, combine ¾ cup salt (rather than 1 cup kosher salt) with 1 gallon of water. Many smoker veterans simplify the brining process by adding enough salt to a gallon of water that will float an egg. Dissolve the salt a little at a time until an egg floats in the solution. You can then add sugar, herbs and other dry ingredients, but don't dilute the liquid-to-salt ratio.

I've brined just about every type of meat and fish, including salmon, Thanksgiving turkeys, venison roasts, and small game birds such as quail and doves. They can all benefit from some time in a brine.

BASIC BRINE

INGREDIENTS

- 1 gallon water
- 1 cup kosher salt
- 1 cup brown sugar
- ¼ cup onion powder
- ¼ cup garlic powder
- ⅓ cup Italian seasoning
- 2 tablespoons black pepper

1. In a saucepan, mix 2 cups of the water with the kosher salt, and heat while stirring until salt is dissolved. In a large, deep container, add warmed salt solution to remaining ingredients. Place venison in brine, and refrigerate overnight. Rinse meat, pat dry and discard brine.

BASIC RUB

There's no such thing as the "perfect" rub. It's a matter of personal preference. Some like it sweet, some like it spicy. Others are fine with salt and pepper. Keep in mind that no matter how long you leave the rub on the meat, it will not penetrate deep into the meat past the first ¼ inch or so. I'll often mix my dry rubs with olive oil to add fat and help distribute the dry seasoning.

Start with the basic rub recipe below, and add other ingredients to create your own signature rub. When it's time to put the rub to work, rub it into every nook and cranny. For a more pronounced flavor, wrap the meat with plastic wrap, and refrigerate it for a day or two before smoking.

INGREDIENTS

- ½ cup kosher or sea salt
- ¼ cup sugar
- 1 teaspoon onion powder
- 1 teaspoon garlic powder
- 1 teaspoon black pepper
- 1 teaspoon paprika

Cures

Curing meat before smoking will enhance the flavor and preserve the meat. The preservation part really isn't all that critical these days because we all have refrigerators. The basic cure is just a combination of salt and sugar. Other cures, such as "No. 1 pink swalt," also called Prague powder, contain sodium nitrate or sodium nitrite, which are used to preserve meats and give them their reddish color when cooked. If you're worried about nitrates and nitrites and don't mind a slice of gray meat, leave them out of the cure, and just use kosher salt or sea salt and sugar. Morton Tender Quick is the most widely distributed commercial cure. It's a salt-based cure that also contains sugar, sodium nitrite and sodium nitrate. Most game processors also stock meat cures for the home chef.

Combine equal parts light brown sugar and kosher salt. Add other flavors like garlic powder, dried herbs and perhaps something spicy like cayenne pepper, and rub it over a trimmed venison roast or muscle. Wrap it in plastic wrap, and refrigerate for 12 to 48 hours, depending on the size of the hunk of meat. Place the meat into a 225-degree smoker, and remove at an internal temperature of 135 to 140 degrees for medium-rare. Tougher cuts, such as necks and shoulders, should be cooked to an internal temperature of 185 to 190 degrees. For fall-off-the-bone tenderness, slather the cooked meat in barbecue sauce, and wrap well in foil before returning it to the smoker for another couple of hours. That's when the "magic" happens, and the lean, tough meat transforms into shredded, moist morsels of deliciousness.

Curing is really necessary only if you plan on cold-smoking, which is smoking meats at temperatures less than 100 degrees, a slow process I rarely use on red meats. The curing process will greatly reduce — but won't necessarily guarantee — any tainting of meat from bacteria. Although a cure is not necessary for smoking meats, it will enhance flavor and color. A typical dry cure has 4 pounds salt, 1½ pounds sugar, 1 ounce sodium nitrate and ¼ ounce sodium nitrite. Measure all ingredients carefully, especially the sodium nitrite. Too much sodium nitrite is toxic. If you're worried about glowing in the dark after ingesting too much of a good thing, purchase a seasoned cure from a reputable source. In general, use about 1 ounce of cure per pound of meat and about a week in the fridge per inch of thickness.

If you find that you really have to know more about curing meats before smoking, there are numerous resources for more information. Start with your local game processor, or purchase cure mixes made specifically for wild game. But remember that smoking venison is really as simple as seasoning the meat and smoking at 200 to 225 degrees until it's done.

Smoked Burger

Firing up the smoker isn't always convenient, like in the dead of winter or when you're just short on time. Here's a way to give you smoke-flavored burgers anytime. You can slap these smoke-flavored venison patties right on a hot grill or freeze them for later. To freeze, place smoked patties on a lightly greased pan or baking sheet, and freeze for 2 hours. Place wax paper squares between patties, and place in a zipper lock freezer-safe bag or, better, vacuum-package for extended freezer storage.

6 ½-pound patties

INGREDIENTS

- 2 cups ground venison
- 1 cup ground beef
- 1 egg, lightly beaten
- 1 cup onion, minced
- 1 tablespoon whole grain mustard
- 2 tablespoon fresh rosemary leaves, minced
- 1 teaspoon garlic powder
- 1 teaspoon paprika
- 1½ teaspoons kosher salt
- ½ teaspoon pepper

1. Combine all ingredients in a medium bowl and mix well (with hands). Divide mixture in half, and make 3 equal balls out of each portion. Press down firmly, and compress into patties, about ¾ inch thick. Place patties in the refrigerator for 2 hours to firm up.

2. Place in a 200- to 225-degree smoker for 30 minutes. Patties can be transferred to a hot grill and cooked until done or cooled completely and frozen for later use. Frozen smoked burgers can be placed on a medium-hot grill or skillet and cooked to desired internal temperature.

Jalapeno, Garlic and Lime Summer Sausage

I'm told that it's called "summer sausage" because it can be stored without refrigeration because of the curing process. I keep my summer sausage in the refrigerator or freezer anyway. I've also made various forms of wild-game summer sausage using only salt as a curing agent. Some people like big hunks of cheese in their summer sausage. Not me. Because I often serve sliced venison summer sausage with fruit and cheese, it seems a bit redundant to have blobs of cheese in the sausage.

This recipe is simplified for those of us who do not own a meat grinder. If you have ever used a cheap meat grinder, you know that they aren't worth much. Plan on spending at least $150, but probably more, for a good one that will actually grind meat. If you have venison scraps rather than ground meat, you can chop them up into small pieces and pulse in a food processor before mixing with the other ingredients.

2 sausages

INGREDIENTS

- ¾ cup cold water
- ¼ cup freshly squeezed lime juice
- 3 tablespoons curing mixture (like Morton® Tender Quick® or Hi Mountain cures)
- 2 teaspoons mustard seed
- 1 teaspoon coarse ground black pepper
- ½ teaspoon ground cumin
- 2¼ pounds ground venison
- ¾ pound ground pork
- 3 jalapeno peppers, seeded and minced
- 5 garlic cloves, minced
- 1 cup cilantro leaves, minced

1. In a large bowl, combine water, lime juice, curing mixture, mustard seed, pepper and cumin, and stir until blended and dissolved. Mix in the ground venison, pork, jalapeno, garlic and cilantro until mixture is tacky, about 3 to 4 minutes.

Pulled Shoulder or Neck Roast

Here's my take on smoking venison shoulder and neck roasts. The beauty of it is that with only minimal effort, you can change, sinewy, bone-in roasts into something of beauty. It's not an exact method. If the meat doesn't fall off the bone, keep smoking.

INGREDIENTS

- 1 venison neck or shoulder roast, bone in or out
- olive oil
- salt and pepper
- barbecue sauce, your favorite

1. Don't bother boning it out. Rub the roast liberally with olive oil, salt and pepper (or your favorite rub). Wrap it with plastic wrap, and refrigerate for at least 12 hours.
2. Place in a 200- to 225-degree smoker for 6 to 8 hours. Meat should pull away from but not fall off of the roast with minimal effort. If it still seems a bit tough, keep smoking.
3. Place roast on two layers of heavy-duty foil. Pour a cup or so of barbecue sauce over and wrap snugly. Place back in the smoker for another 3 to 4 hours or until meat falls off the bone.

SERVING SUGGESTIONS

✔ Shred meat, place in a soft bun, and top with creamy coleslaw.

✔ Season with Southwestern spices, and stuff into tacos, enchiladas and tamales.

✔ Toss with avocado and fresh tomato salsa, and fold into an omelette.

✔ Serve on Hawaiian sweet rolls as an appetizer.

✔ Combine with pinto beans, onions, peppers and tomato sauce.

Sweet-Hot Jerky

Based on a casual observation of my hunting buddy's jerky choices, I'd say that sweet-and hot-flavored jerky is about even with teriyaki. Turning venison into jerky is a natural. It's lean, practically devoid of fat, and dries out faster than beef. The meat has to be trimmed of all visible silver skin, sinew and anything that's not muscle. How you slice the meat will directly affect the chewability of the jerky. Meat has a distinct grain. Slicing across the grain makes it more tender. Slicing with the grain will make it last longer, but you might get a sore jaw if it's cut too thick. About ⅛ to ¼ inch is perfect.

For 2 pounds of venison, about 4 cups

INGREDIENTS

- 1 cup soy sauce
- ¼ cup Worcestershire sauce
- ¼ cup kosher salt
- ¼ cup brown sugar
- 1 tablespoon freshly ground black pepper
- 1 tablespoon garlic powder
- 1 teaspoon cayenne pepper

1. Slice meat as thinly as possible. If needed, lightly pound meat until of even thickness. Combine soy sauce and Worcestershire sauce in a medium bowl, add sliced meat, and toss to coat evenly. Cover and refrigerate for 12 to 24 hours. Remove meat from marinade, and pat dry.

2. Combine kosher salt with remaining ingredients. Coat meat evenly, and stack sliced game one on top of the other. Wrap with plastic wrap, and refrigerate for 12 hours.

3. Dry on racks in a 200-degree smoker. Average drying time is 2 to 3 hours, depending on meat thickness.

Note: Jerky stored for more than a couple of weeks should be properly packaged and frozen.

Lettuce Cups with Smoked Venison

Wrapping food in lettuce wraps has made a big impression on the dining public. These are cool and crisp on the outside and warm, crunchy and smoky on the inside. The best way to serve lettuce cups is family style. Stack lettuce leaves, filling and condiments like Asian hot sauce, hoisin sauce and soy sauce on the side.

Making intact lettuce cups out of a head of iceberg lettuce can be tricky. When choosing your lettuce at the store, buy the lightest, loosest heads that can be broken apart easily without tearing the leaves. Allow one head of lettuce for 2 or 3 people. Start by removing the stem end. Remove the lettuce leaves from the thicker stem end, and work them into separate leaves. For company, I trim the ragged leaves into symmetrical same-sized cups. Save the trim and cores for salads. Most people can eat 4 to 6 filled cups.

6 servings

INGREDIENTS

- 2 pounds venison steaks, trimmed
- ¼ cup low-sodium soy sauce
- ½ teaspoon Asian sesame oil

FILLING

- 2 tablespoons olive oil
- ½ teaspoon Asian sesame oil
- ½ cup carrot, peeled and finely diced
- ½ cup celery stalk, finely diced
- 3 tablespoons low-sodium soy sauce
- 2 tablespoons orange juice concentrate
- 2 garlic cloves, minced
- 4 green onions, minced
- ½ cup water chestnuts, diced
- 2 tablespoons pickled ginger, minced (or substitute 1 tablespoon fresh peeled and minced ginger root)
- 1½ cups cooked rice, white or brown
- 3 to 4 heads iceberg lettuce (look for heads that are loose, not firm and tight)
- Sriracha sauce
- hoisin sauce

1. Place meat in a container or zipper-lock bag. Add soy sauce and sesame oil, and toss to coat. Refrigerate for 2 to 4 hours. Remove meat from refrigerator, and let rest at room temperature for 20 minutes. Place in a 250-degree smoker for 25 minutes or until meat is medium-rare (about 135 degrees). Cool and chop meat into pea-sized pieces.

2. Heat olive and sesame oil in a large wok or skillet over medium-high heat. Add carrot and celery, and stir-fry for 3 minutes. Add chopped venison, soy sauce and next 6 ingredients. Cook until warmed throughout. Transfer mixture into 4 bowls, and serve with lettuce cups, Sriracha and hoisin sauces.

3. To assemble lettuce cups, spread a very thin layer of hoisin sauce on the center of a lettuce cup. Spoon a few tablespoons of the meat mixture into the lettuce, and add a drop or two of Sriracha for spicy heat. Hold the lettuce cup firmly, and eat from one end to the other.